The Toilet Paper Tigers

GORDON KORMAN

The Toilet Paper Tigers

SCHOLASTIC HARDCOVER

Scholastic Inc.
New York

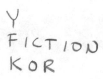

Y
FICTION
KOR

Library of Congress Cataloging-in-Publication Data

Korman, Gordon.
    The Toilet Paper Tigers / by Gordon Korman.
197 p.   cm.
    Summary: When his Little League team gets a coach who knows nothing about baseball, seventh-grader Corey is dismayed to see the team taken over by the coach's pushy twelve-year-old granddaughter.

ISBN 0-590-46230-X

    [1. Baseball — Fiction.   2. Humorous stories.]   I. Title.
PZ7.K8369To   1993
[Fic] — dc20   92-27277
                                                                   CIP
                                                                    AC

12 11 10 9 8 7 6 5 4 3 2 1   3 4 5 6 7 8/9

Printed in the U.S.A.   37

First Scholastic printing, August 1993

For the 1992 World Series Champion
Toronto Blue Jays,
and the fans of the 1977 Jays,
who cheered even when there was no light
at the end of the tunnel.

CONTENTS

The
Toilet
Paper
Tigers

CHAPTER ◇1◇

Coach —
Professor Pendergast

Our coach had a great mind for science, but he was a total goose-egg when it came to baseball. I still can't figure out what would make a sixty-year-old guy who worked in a particle accelerator (whatever that is) want to coach Little League — and then forget to show up the day they were drafting players. By the time Professor Pendergast made it to the coaches' meeting, there were exactly nine players left — us. The Feather-Soft Tigers, sponsored by Feather-Soft Bathroom Tissue Inc. Didn't it kind of figure? The warmed-over leftovers of the league were going to be the toilet paper team. All coached by a man who thought a foul ball was a line drive into some farmer's manure spreader.

Everybody in Spooner loved Professor Pendergast. The particle accelerator was great for the town, and all the employees agreed that there was no nicer boss than our coach. So we were pretty thrilled to be Tigers — at first. Even when the professor told us our uniforms weren't ready, nobody thought it was a big deal. Hey, one practice in sweats never killed anybody.

Only there was no practice. Nobody even said the word *baseball*. Instead, our coach talked about the lepton, which is this science thing that he's supposed to be an authority on.

"What do they look like?" I asked. Not because I cared, but because the sooner we got all this lepton stuff out of the way, the sooner we could start playing.

"Oh, you can't see a lepton," the professor explained. "Not even with an electron microscope. They're far too tiny."

"If you can't see it, how do you know it's there?" asked Kevin Featherstone. His dad owned Feather-Soft Bathroom Tissue Inc.

The professor glowed. You could tell he really got into this physics stuff. "In the particle accelerator, we can create collisions that produce leptons that last for as long as three one-billionths of a second!"

In other words, he was a professor of nothing. He sure wasn't a professor of baseball.

"So," I ventured, "who do you think is going to be our leadoff batter?"

Professor Pendergast looked at me like I was some kind of idiot. "Well, I imagine it will have to be one of you boys," he replied, and the conversation switched back to leptons.

Tim Laredo shot me a nervous look. Tim and I, and Tuba Dave Jablonski were the only three guys who had played Little League before. Okay, we weren't experts, but we were pretty sure this wasn't what you should be doing in the very first practice.

I decided to take another stab at mentioning you-know-what. "How about a practice game?" I suggested.

Our coach brightened further. "Excellent idea!" He pointed in the general direction of the field. "Now, some of you boys go all the way out there — uh, some of you go partway out there and the rest of you — well, uh, stay here."

We stared at him.

"Don't you even know the positions?" asked Tim.

The professor pointed to home plate. "I know that pentagonal surface is significant — " He scratched his head. "Hmmm . . ."

"Well — " I didn't want to be rude, but somebody had to ask! "Why did you sign up to be a coach when you don't know anything about baseball?"

"My granddaughter is going to be staying with me for the summer," he admitted. "And I thought this would be a good way to get to know some young people . . ." His voice trailed off. Maybe he

3

finally realized that it wasn't exactly fair to turn our whole season into garbage so some girl wouldn't be bored. "I'm sorry — "

I should've been on my way home to convince my parents to demand our money back. But Professor Pendergast looked really upset and I thought — here was the guy who'd done so much for our town. A renowned genius living in Spooner, Texas, but was he ever snobby or stuck-up? No! And *we* were mad because he didn't know much about baseball.

All of a sudden I heard myself bellowing, "Three cheers for Professor Pendergast!"

We hip-hip-hoorayed ourselves hoarse, and the professor was so happy he loaded us all up into his minivan, and took us to the Six Flags Amusement Park. He gorged us with hot dogs and cotton candy and took us on the Enormo-Coaster. It was fun. It was *great*. But it wasn't baseball.

Only a third of us threw up.

At our next practice the *professor* didn't even show up! When I got there, the only other person around was this girl. She was about my age, with blonde hair, and wore Day-Glo orange sunglasses, a New York City T-shirt, army fatigues, and pink high-tops.

She flipped up her sunglasses and barked, "Name!"

"Uh — Corey Johnson," I said, mystified. "Where's Professor Pendergast?"

"Oh, P.P.'s going to be late. He's showing some Korean scientists around the particle accelerator. I'm handling things until he gets here."

"Who are you?"

She grinned broadly, and held out her hand. "Kristy Pendergast. 'Tsup?"

" 'Tsup?' " I repeated, shaking her hand weakly. It took me half the season to figure out that 'tsup was Kristy's way of saying *what's up?* which, I think, meant *hello*.

"Yeah! How you doin'? *Que pasa?* What's shakin'? How's it goin'? 'Tsup?"

I jumped on the only thing that made sense. "Pendergast?" Then I remembered why our coach volunteered for his job in the first place. "You're the professor's granddaughter!" I said, snapping my fingers.

"Word," she approved.

I stared at her. "Word?"

"You know, check, *sí,* affirmative! Yes," she added when she saw my mouth drop open in total confusion. "I'm visiting for a few months. I'm from New York, dude! The parental units are doing the Europe thing this summer, so I'm chilling out down here with my main man P.P. Now — Johnson — Johnson — " She checked her clipboard. "Okay, you're starting in left field."

"What?" I blurted. "I'm a pitcher!"

Kristy shrugged sympathetically. "So's this kid Kevin Featherstone. Sorry, bro'."

"But shouldn't we hold a tryout to see who's better?" I demanded.

"Earth to Johnson; Earth to Johnson," Kristy chanted. "Featherstone's the sponsor. He puts up the bucks — his kid plays where he likes."

I couldn't believe it. "Mr. Featherstone said that?"

Kristy was shaking her head and clucking sadly. "You just don't get it, do you? You rural dudes expect life to be fair. You should spend a few days in New York. Reality sandwich, man. Left field."

At that moment, Kevin showed up. "You're the pitcher," I told him, choking on my reality sandwich.

"Yo, Featherstone," Kristy greeted him. " 'Tsup? Kristy Pendergast. I'm in charge here."

Notice how she promoted herself from "handling things" to "in charge"? Well, by the time the Tigers were all there, she was "assistant manager," "batting coach," "trainer," and "public relations chief."

I have to admit she was fair. She was just as annoying to everyone else as she was to me. Ernie MacIntosh's glove was too small; Luis Bono was the catcher and should have been wearing cleats;

6

Caspar Howard's socks were drooping; this wasn't right; that wasn't right; they do it better in New York; blah, blah, blah. I sat there, burning inside. Who died and left her king? I was just about ready to start a dugout revolt when the professor walked in.

"Grandpa! You got here just in time! That's terrific!"

The professor's face lit up at just the sight of her. "How's my little princess? Have you been getting along with my team?"

"Oh, yes, Grandpa!" she smiled sweetly. "We're all great friends!"

Wait a minute. What happened to *yo,* and *'tsup,* and *P.P. my main man*? It looked like, when the professor was around, the reality sandwich turned into a snow-job casserole.

The first order of business was our uniforms, which were ready at last. They were white, with FEATHER-SOFT TIGERS printed in blue. Between the words was a roll of toilet paper. On each sheet was a picture of a tiger holding a baseball bat.

We all packed into the washroom hut to get changed.

"Can you believe that girl?" I complained. "Bad enough that our coach is a zero, now we have to put up with Kristy!"

"Why does she talk like that?" asked Ernie Mac-Intosh.

"Oh, she's much cooler than us!" I said sarcastically. "She's from New York. All New Yorkers talk that way."

"No wonder New York has so many problems," Ernie decided. "No one can figure out what anybody else is saying."

Tim pulled off his sweatpants. "Hey, you don't think that, since the professor can't really do it, Kristy might try to coach us herself?"

"No!" I exclaimed in horror. "Absolutely not! Under no circumstances is that girl — "

Suddenly, there was a click and a brilliant flash blinded us. When the dots cleared away from my eyes I saw it. A camera was stuck in through the open door. *And we were all standing around the bathroom in our jockstraps!*

I cried out, "Hey — " but the hand disappeared. The door shut behind it.

We suited up in seconds and rushed outside to find Kristy patting her camera.

"What'd you do that for?" bawled Ernie.

She was totally calm. "Yo, man, haven't you ever heard of team pictures?" She snickered. "I hope I got everybody's good side."

"Give me that camera!" I snarled through clenched teeth.

She frowned. "I heard you in there dissing my main man P.P."

"Dissing?" I repeated.

"Disrespecting!" she translated. "Somebody has to keep you jerks in line."

"You think you can push us around because you've got a picture of — of *that*?"

"Not at all." She replaced the lens cap on her camera. "Of course, you guys wouldn't want a picture like this to fall into the wrong hands — "

"Not our mothers!" blurted Tuba Dave in agony.

I lunged for the camera but Kristy deftly held it just outside my grasp. "No more cracks about my main man P.P." she said firmly.

"Well, he isn't exactly a baseball expert!" I said feelingly.

"You know, you dudes are all starting junior high this September." Kristy mused. "Wouldn't it be *unfortunate* if a copy of this picture just so happened to get pasted on every locker in the school?"

My breath caught in my throat. A gasp of horror rose from my fellow Tigers. We'd all heard rumors about how tough it was to be a seventh grader at Spooner Junior High. If Kristy's picture got around, we'd be laughingstocks!

I looked her straight in the eye. "You don't have the nerve."

She laughed in my face. "Get real, bro. I'm from New York."

Ernie was the first to crack. "What do we have to do?"

"Check it out," she replied. "My main man P.P.'s

a great guy. But his head is all balled up with lep-tons and stuff. So it's been a long time since his last chow-fest with the reality sandwich."

Unbelievably, I thought I understood. "Well, at least we agree on one thing," I said grudgingly. "We all like the coach. But when it comes to baseball, he's hopeless."

"He doesn't expect the World Series," she went on. "He just wants a normal team — win a few, lose a few, have some fun. Dig?"

"And we would be thrilled to oblige," I said sar-castically. "I'm pretty sure we can handle the 'lose a few' part. But we may need a little help with the 'win a few,' like maybe some experienced coach-ing."

"You don't need experience! You've got the ul-timate advantage! All the competition is from Spooner, and all the other one-horse towns around here. But the Tigers are running on brain power that's straight from New York!"

There was a babble of protest.

I said, "Forget it, Kristy. Nobody's going to let you coach this team."

"Hey!" she said. "Cool your jets. Mellow out. Calm down. Take five. Make like a melon and chill. I'm just a fan. An interested party. A sports buff. A booster."

Then she patted her camera, and it made me think of the picture that was held inside, locked on a piece of film. I thought back to the washroom. How had I been standing? Could you see my face? What else (gulp!) could you see?

"Well, what are we waiting for?" I announced. "Let's practice."

Professor Pendergast was about as useful as air-conditioning in the Arctic. It would be unfair to say he didn't know which end of the bat to hold. He did. (The thin end.) But when Tim Laredo popped one straight up a thousand miles, our coach considered it a home run. He thought a hit was anything that made contact with the bat, including the "hit" that ends up in the bleachers behind you, the "hit" where you never make it to first, and the "hit" that somebody catches. Bobby Ray walloped a monster home run that was out of the park by half a block. Professor Pendergast thought it was a passed ball.

"At least that's a baseball word," Tim told me in the field. "When I dropped a long fly, he called it a touchdown, 'cause it touched the ground."

Kristy, our "booster," was a pain in the butt. She started out in charge of equipment, but somewhere in there, she found time to bug everybody on the whole team. She drove me so crazy about my batting stance that I actually threatened to beat her over the head with the bat. I am *not* a violent person!

"Yo, man," was Kristy's mild comment. "You say something like that to a New Yorker, you've got to be prepared to do it."

"I've never been to New York." I told her. "But if it's full of eight million people like you, it must be the worst place on Earth."

Ernie pulled me aside. "What are you — crazy?" he hissed. "You can't talk to her like that! If she gets mad she'll develop The Picture!"

"Don't be stupid," I said peevishly. "You want to be her slave for life?"

"I can't remember exactly when the flash went off," moaned Luis. "I might have been bending over to tie my shoes."

"What a day to wear bunny rabbit underwear!" added Bobby Ray.

"What do you care?" Tim asked him. "You go to school in Eaton."

Bobby Ray shook his head. "Eaton Junior High comes to Spooner for shop and home ec. I'm dead."

"I sure hope my birthmark doesn't show," put in Tuba Dave.

"What birthmark?" asked Ernie.

"Well, you can't see it *now*!" Tuba Dave exploded.

What a practice! Six of us couldn't hit. Four of us couldn't catch. Nobody could handle a routine grounder. And when Kevin was on the mound, no one was safe! Talk about wild! He didn't just bean the batters; he nailed me in the on-deck circle!

"Sorry," Kevin called.

Before chewing him out, I reminded myself that this was probably the guy's dream. Why else would he get his dad to pull strings to make him pitcher?

"I guess this really means a lot to you," I commented, tossing him the ball. "Pitching, I mean."

Kevin looked surprised. "Not really."

I frowned. "Well, then, I guess your dad's the one who wants you to pitch."

He shrugged. "Dad doesn't care. He just wants me to be part of the team. Actually, I thought *you* were going to be our pitcher."

By the time I found Kristy, my face was burning hot, and it had nothing to do with the weather.

" 'Tsup, Johnson? You look a little purple. Grape City, man."

Mutiny City. "Kevin doesn't care who pitches!" I rasped. "Kevin's *father* doesn't care who pitches! You lied!"

"Chill out," she said blandly.

But by then, the professor was on the scene. "What's the trouble, Princess?"

I was triumphant. Now Kristy couldn't shoot me down without showing her grandfather what a tyrant she was.

"I think I should get the chance to try out for pitcher," I said.

The professor beamed. "Of course!" He pointed to the outfield, where some of the guys had paired up to play catch. "See? Everybody's pitching. You pitch to your partner, and then he pitches back to you."

"But that's not pitching!" I protested. "That's throwing!"

"Well, perhaps you can try out for thrower," suggested our coach. And he walked away, leaving Kristy grinning so wide — I can still see it in my mind. It almost killed me.

"You won't get away with this," I told her, my eyes mere slits.

Kristy was totally calm. "I'm considering becoming a photographer when I grow up. What do you think? Do I take great pictures, or what?"

I was so furious that I couldn't be trusted with a bat. I went to sit in the bleachers. It was too painful to watch the practice, so I watched the professor. He was smiling and applauding, while the guys scrambled around like chickens with their heads cut off. He didn't even know enough about baseball to realize this wasn't it!

Finally, when the whole disaster was over he said, "Boys, I'm very proud of you."

Kristy came over, smiling her used car salesman smile. "Wasn't that a wonderful practice, Grandpa?" To me she whispered, "Yo, man, you guys need help!"

◇

By midnight, I still hadn't cooled down. I lay in my bed shaking with rage. Kristy hadn't even been in town a whole day yet, and already my summer was ruined!

The worst part was there was nothing we could do about it! The guys would never dare go up against her because they were so spooked by The Picture. That meant we also couldn't get our parents to complain. She'd blame us and develop the film. And trying to explain anything to the professor was impossible. He'd never believe the truth about his "little princess." We were trapped, unless . . .

I jumped up and ran to my desk. Maybe *we* couldn't stop Kristy Pendergast, but if the League complained, the professor would have to do something. I found my league pamphlet and checked the name and address of the president.

Dear Mr. Lopez,

I think you should know that a terrible person named Kristy Pendergast is ruining the Feather-Soft Tigers by bossing everybody around, and not letting peo-

*ple pitch. She is the granddaughter of
the coach, who is a really nice guy, except he thinks she's great. Please help.
The whole team is going down the
drain.*

Signed,

Anonymous

I sat back and reread my letter with satisfaction. When Mr. Lopez read this, he'd make the professor tell Kristy to mind her own business. And the beauty of it was that Kristy would never know who did her in.

I went back to bed and slept like a baby.

CHAPTER ⟨2⟩

Catcher — Luis Bono

No one thought it was a big deal when our catcher, Luis Bono, took a fastball right in the mask during the warm-up before our first game.

Actually, we were all kind of impressed that Kevin had managed to get one over the plate. The ball sizzled in from the mound, hitting the gap in the bars of the mask right between Luis's eyes. There was a muffled *twang,* and the ball stuck there, jammed in the mask.

"Yo, bro', looks like a giant insect eye! Attack of the praying mantises!" laughed Kristy.

I took comfort in my letter to the League president, which had gone out yesterday.

Wouldn't you know it? Professor Pendergast, the brilliant lepton scientist, couldn't figure out how to get a baseball out from between the bars of a catcher's mask. And it was really in there. Even Tuba Dave, our strongest player, couldn't pull it out.

"Did anybody get the license number of that truck?" asked Luis, dazed.

"What a bunch of hicks!" exclaimed Kristy, pulling a hairpin out of her ponytail. She grabbed the mask from Tuba Dave's hands, jammed the hairpin under the ball and, with a twist of the wrist, it was all over. The ball popped out, play ball.

Our opponents were Chet's Texaco Oilers from across town. Kristy started out by humiliating us, mounting a cardboard sign on top of her grandfather's van. It read:

OILERS STINK

Mr. Rudolph, the umpire, made the professor take it down, and we got an official warning. We were in agony since Mr. Rudolph was vice principal of Spooner Junior High. I was sort of hoping to get on his good side. That way I could warn him to take down the eight hundred photographs of a baseball team in their jockstraps that just *might* show up on Day One of school. But now he was mad at all the Tigers, thanks to Guess Who.

"Oh, I didn't do it, Grandpa," said Kristy innocently. And our coach, a great scientific mind, believed her. She still had red paint on her hands!

Our parents got to see all this, since the spectators were beginning to arrive. *Every guy* whose folks were there got the old "poor sportsmanship" lecture after the game. So none of us were upset that only twenty people showed up — mostly parents and brothers and sisters of the two teams.

It wasn't exactly the World Series. The other team stank, but you couldn't smell them over the reek that was coming from us.

The Oilers started at bat, and we knew we were in trouble early. On the first pitch, Luis saw a ball coming at him and went a little nuts. He dove out of the way, knocking Mr. Rudolph flying.

"Okay, kid," panted the umpire, scrambling to his feet and dusting himself off. "Calm down."

But the second pitch produced the same result. This time, Luis tackled the batter, who jumped up and was ready to make a big deal out of it.

"What are you — crazy, kid?"

"*Me* crazy?!" cried Luis. "You were supposed to hit that!"

The batter and Mr. Rudolph both regarded Luis oddly. Kristy stuck her nose into it, which was like running up to a fire with a bucket of gasoline.

" 'Tsup, dudes? Luis, you okay?"

Outraged, our catcher pointed at Kevin on the mound. "He keeps throwing those right *at* me!"

"He's the pitcher, stupid!" growled the batter. "And you're the catcher!"

Kristy gazed at him blandly. "Are you going to

shut up now, or only after I pull your right nostril back and hook it over the button on your left hip pocket?"

Mr. Rudolph stared at her. "Who *are* you?"

And Kristy retreated into the dugout.

Ever wonder if a baseball game could be played without a catcher? Luis ducked, dove, leapt, and rolled, and not a single throw reached his mitt. We allowed eighteen stolen bases! There were so many runners out there, it looked like a track meet! Luis's mom even came out onto the field to try to calm her son down. It didn't help.

At one point, in the second inning, with the Oilers up at bat and leading 3–zip, bases loaded, Luis saw a fastball in flight and covered his mask with his mitt. The ball bounced off his chest pad right onto the plate. The guy scoring from third almost killed himself on it. Ernie MacIntosh charged in from first base, too late to tag the next guy coming home, so he tried to throw to third. I got this ball in left field. The Oilers scored a grand slam without a hit! All errors! I wonder if that's ever been done before.

"Splendid! Splendid!" was the professor's comment.

Our coach pretty much cheered his way through the whole thing. It was too bad that he went to the bathroom in the bottom of the fourth because he missed our hit. Bobby Ray Devereaux managed to smack a line drive between the shortstop and the third baseman. Bobby Ray got greedy, though, and went for second base. He was out by a mile, but Kristy launched off the bench like a Polaris missile.

"Kristy!" I hissed. *"No!"*

Too late. "What are you — *crazy*, Ump?" she howled, kicking dirt all over Mr. Rudolph's shoes. "You're missing a great game here! Get some glasses!"

By the time the professor got back, his sweet little granddaughter was in the parking lot, ejected in disgrace.

"Where's Kristy?" he asked.

There were a lot of "ums" and "uhs," because nobody wanted to tell the hero of Spooner that his little princess was Godzilla.

"She — uh — went out to get some air," Ernie improvised. Ernie was not known for his ability to think under pressure.

Then, believe it or not, the game got stupider. Tuba Dave popped straight up, and the ball came down and hit him on the head. So his folks escorted him home with a headache. Since we only had nine guys to start with, we had to borrow a second baseman from the other team. We complained that the new kid wouldn't be trying a hundred percent. But even I have to admit that he was our best player. He almost set up a double play, except that Ernie missed the perfect throw to first, and the play turned into an inside-the-park home run. Well, sort of inside-the-park, because the ball rolled under the bleachers into some high grass, and we couldn't find it.

After twenty minutes of searching, the other team wanted to go home. So Mr. Rudolph called the game in the fifth inning. Final score: Oilers 9, Tigers 0.

"Boys, you did splendidly well," beamed Professor Pendergast.

"But, Coach," I protested, "we got creamed!"

"It's not whether you win or lose," proclaimed our coach. "It's how you play the game." Ever wonder why they never say that to the guys who win?

"But we didn't play well either," Tim pointed out. "We didn't just lose. We stank and lost. We're hopeless."

"Even my dad walked out," added Caspar.

The coach surveyed our long faces in genuine alarm. "You're not having fun."

It was amazing. Our chances of ever even scoring a run, let alone winning a game, were way below zero. Yet all we could think of was how upset Professor Pendergast looked.

"Of course we had fun," I lied and forced myself to smile. "It was — a blast."

"Yeah!" Kevin enthused. "Sure, we didn't get any runs, but we had some — uh — interesting defensive plays."

The professor wasn't convinced. So we had to

celebrate our terrific disaster. We gave him a cheering escort to the parking lot. The other team thought we were nuts.

There wasn't much finger-pointing or name-calling. Nobody accused anyone else of being the goat; we were all goats. But I figured Luis had to be at least the leader of the herd.

"What happened to him?" I asked after our catcher had jogged home. "He was fine at practice."

It took Kristy to remember the incident during the warm-up. "You hayseeds know nothing about psychology," she explained. "He's gun-shy from that fastball he almost ate."

"But he had a mask on!" I protested.

"He still got it right between the eyes, man! When he sees a baseball on the way, it brings it all back!"

"But he's our only catcher!" wailed Tim.

"The mind is a delicate thing," lectured Dr. Kristy Freud, famed New York psychiatrist. "We can't just say 'Get over it, or else.' It could turn him into a vegetable!"

"Really?" Tim was wide-eyed.

She nodded intently. "Or he could snap the other way — like one of those guys from the movies, with a chain saw!"

"Aw, come on! This is stupid!" I protested. "We've all known Luis for years! He's not going to start going after people with chain saws just because he got a ball in the face!"

"His father owns that equipment rental place," put in Ernie worriedly. "He could get a chain saw easy."

"We have to be gentle," Kristy decided, "build up his confidence, show him we care. We'll help him with his problem, but we'll make sure not to put any pressure on him."

"Our next game is in three days," I pointed out.

"Oh, well, if he's not cured by then, he's dead meat," said Kristy.

◇

Stage One of the plan, according to Kristy, was me.

"*Me!?* Why *me*?"

"You're his teammate, his trusted friend," she insisted.

"We're not best friends! We happen to be neighbors!" I protested. "If I bang on his door and ask to have a catch, it'll be the first time ever! He'll think I'm nuts!"

She rapped on my head with her clenched fist. "Hello? Anybody home? We've got to get Luis to admit he has a problem before we can treat it. If you guys are tossing a ball around, you can start making like a pitcher, throwing harder and harder, until it brings out the old fear."

"What's so great about that?" I demanded. "The old fear cost us a ball game."

She rolled her eyes. "Then we have an open rap session. You know — hey, Luis, 'tsupwitchoo?"

'Tsupwitchoo? It took me a while but I nailed it down: What's up with you?

I figured it was okay to go along with Kristy here. After all, the Tigers sure wouldn't get any better with a catcher who was afraid of the ball.

We walked together over to Luis's place, and I rang the bell. I glanced over to Kristy for reassurance, and she was gone.

"Psssst! Over here." She was crouched in the middle of a honeysuckle bush, flashing me the thumbs-up signal.

"Get back out here!" I rasped. But by then, Luis was at the door. "Oh, hi," I said, grinning like a jackass. "I just wondered if you wanted to have a catch."

"Not really," said Luis.

Like a computer, my mind raced through Kristy's instructions. There was nothing to cover "not really." "Hang on a second. I've got to go talk to this bush."

Kristy jumped out into the open. "Hey, Luis, 'tsup? Johnson and I thought maybe you've got something you want to tell us."

"About what?"

She shrugged expansively. "*Any* subject. World politics! Black holes! Stamp collecting! Why you can't catch a baseball worth beans — "

"Cut it out!" I exploded. "Look, Luis, we saw you having some problems yesterday. We'd like to help."

Luis looked miserable. "You've got to find someone to replace me."

Kristy shook her head. "No can do, baby. You guys are the last nine losers in this league."

"I can't understand it!" Our catcher looked haunted. "Every time I see the ball coming at me, I figure, 'This is the one that's going to knock my head off!' I had a dream last night. All the best pitchers were there — Roger Clemens, and Nolan Ryan, and Dennis Eckersley, and Dwight Gooden — and they were all throwing at my head!"

"That's cold, man," Kristy sympathized. "But don't sweat it, because we're all in this together. We'll see you through. Just like the Three Musketeers — all for one, and one for all."

On the way back to my place, she curled her lip in disgust. "Sheesh, what a wimp!"

"Hey!" I exploded. "What about the Three Musketeers? What about 'We're all in this together?' "

"Hey, man, Roger Clemens never threw anything at *me*!"

"I'll talk to the professor," I mused. "We could move Luis to left field. You're lucky if you get a ball a week out there, and they sure won't be line drives, and — "

She was shaking her head pityingly. "In New York, you get over your problems by facing up to them, not by hiding out in left field. You pick up the reality sandwich, hold your nose, and take a bite so big you could choke on it, man. That's what Luis has to do!"

"I checked with the luncheonette," I said sarcastically. "They're fresh out of reality. How about liverwurst?"

"Lose the comedy routine," said Kristy. "It's time for Luis to confront his deepest fear."

"Roger Clemens hitting him with a baseball?" I asked incredulously.

"Well, obviously, Roger Clemens isn't going to come to a one-horse town like this." She shrugged. "So I guess you'll have to do it."

"Are you nuts?" I exploded. "I can't just walk up to the guy and bean him with a baseball! It's — assault with a deadly weapon!"

"It's a baseball," she said calmly, "not a hand grenade. And you won't be throwing your hardest. It'll hurt; it may give him a bruise. But the guy'll see he's still alive, and he'll be cured."

"Forget it," I told her and started to walk away.

Kristy reached into her pocket and pulled out a small black film canister. "Hey, Johnson! There's a Fotomat at the mall, right?"

I stopped in my tracks. "What's on that?"

She shrugged. "Family stuff — pictures of my dog, our trip to Niagara Falls, a bunch of naked baseball players — "

"We weren't naked!" I cried out.

"There's one way to find out," she smiled serenely.

"You wouldn't."

In answer, she strolled off in the direction of Spooner Mall. I followed, making a long speech about how the jig was up.

"You want us to think you're so tough? Well, forget it! You're all talk and no action. One hundred percent hot air. I'll bet there wasn't any film in the camera! I'll bet the lens cap was still on! I'll bet the batteries were dead — "

She marched through the crowded mall to the Spooner Fotomat, and handed in her canister.

I was mesmerized by the developing machine. An endless procession of photos passed by the window on the conveyer belt. Practically every shopper paused to check out the pictures. I swallowed hard. In a few short minutes, *we* would be on that conveyer — in our underwear, jockstraps or worse — for full public viewing. And wasn't that my mother's entire bridge club heading this way?

"No-o-o!" I cried out.

The Fotomat guy looked at me like I had a cabbage for a head.

I chickened out totally. "I'll do it! I'll hit Luis with

a baseball!" I babbled at Kristy. "Just don't develop The Picture!"

She snatched back the film, and grinned. "You're the boss, bro'."

◇

Kristy decided that tonight would be the perfect time. Luis always helped out at his father's store in the evenings, and that was when we went to do the deed.

"I hope you can do this," Kristy was warning me. We were crouched between two parked cars in front of Bono's Equipment Rentals. "Don't break the store window! They cost, like, zillions of dollars!"

"Hey," I said sharply. "I'm a pitcher. Just because *somebody* stuck me way out in left field doesn't mean I can't put a ball exactly where I want to."

The look on her face clearly said she didn't think I was that good. And that's when I vowed that I was going to bounce a perfect strike dead center off Luis's forehead.

Inside, Mr. Bono was closing up, so I bore down, just like the big league pitchers. I made the whole universe shrink down to that one little doorway. Then I shrank the doorway down to that one little forehead that was going to be there in a minute. I couldn't miss. It was the only thing in the universe to throw at.

There was the sound of the bells on the door, and the forehead was there! I sprang up, and let fly the perfect pitch — not too hard, not too soft, straight as an arrow.

Direct hit!

Wrong forehead!

Terence Laredo, Tim's sixteen-year-old brother, known to all of us as Terence the Terrorist. He stared at me, veins bulging, one hand clutching his right eye, the other holding — yes, a chain saw.

"Why, you little —"

I didn't hear what he called me, because I was running too hard. And, at that, I was a good three steps behind Kristy.

I should be grateful. When he caught me, he didn't use the chain saw.

" 'Tsup?" panted Kristy, turning to face Terence. "Kristy Pendergast from New York. That's quite a sprint you've got there! Adrenaline city, man! Ever time it without the chain saw?"

"I'm gonna have a black eye because of you!" the Terrorist roared at me from an altitude of about half an inch. He'd had onions for dinner. Yeccch.

"A black eye?" Kristy gazed into his face, which was already starting to swell. "I don't think so. Which eye?"

"This one!" He hauled off and belted me with a hammer punch that almost took my head off.

"Oh, that eye," said Kristy.

The worst part was Luis saw the whole thing, and figured out what we'd been trying to do, and why.

Face it. I should have killed Kristy. But she was the one who dragged me home and made up the story for my parents about how I walked into a door.

"You took it like a man," she praised, holding an ice pack against my eye. "Very New York."

I kicked her out of the house.

The crank call came just before the eleven o'clock news that night. "Come to the game an hour early tomorrow," the muffled voice intoned. "This means you."

"Kristy, why are you bugging me so late?"

"Oh, hi. 'Tsup? I'm just calling to make sure everyone's there, because we're going to cure Luis once and for all."

"What are we going to do?" I snarled, eye throbbing. "Pelt him with spears? Shoot him with a bazooka? Launch a missile down his pants?"

"You'll see." Click.

If it hadn't been so late, I'd have phoned all the guys to tell them not to show up. But the next day, there we were, milling around like sheep, waiting for Kristy's orders. It was amazing what The Picture had done to all of us.

"What happened to your eye?" asked Ernie. My shiner was in full bloom by now.

"Terence the Terrorist attacked me with a chain saw," I replied sourly.

"He came after me, too!" added Tim, wide-eyed. "Because you're my friend! He rubbed my face up and down the carpet, made me eat a shoelace, burned a hole in my jean jacket, and deducted six inches from my half of the room! I got off easy."

" 'Tsup, guys?" Kristy appeared, Luis in tow. "Okay, we all need to form a circle around me and Luis."

"Why?" I asked suspiciously.

From her hip pocket, she produced a well-thumbed paperback entitled *Hypnotism*.

"Aw, come on! That's stupid!" Tim protested. "Hypnotism doesn't work!"

"Yo, man, Luis agreed, so don't hassle it!"

"Yeah," I said bitterly. "Luis agreed because you threatened to develop The Picture."

"*Not* true," Kristy said righteously. "It was pure team loyalty."

It's the Kristy disease. I mean, I'm positive everybody else knew this wasn't going to work. But she just kept shooting her mouth off. And pretty soon, there we were, in the shady part of the clubhouse, sitting around in a circle, hypnotizing Luis.

Guess what she swung back and forth in front of Luis's face! That stupid film canister on a string!

Just in case we needed a little reminder of why we were at her mercy! Then she began to chant, "You are getting sleepy — very sleepy — so-o-o-o sleepy — your eyelids are becoming heavy — your eyes are closing — "

Ernie yawned.

"Not you, stupid!" hissed Tuba Dave.

"Sle-e-e-e-py — sle-e-e-e-py — " Kristy continued. "Now, on the count of three — "

"I'm not hypnotized yet," Luis interrupted.

"Are you sure?" asked Kristy. "You might be hypnotized and not even know it."

Luis shrugged. "I don't think so."

Kristy gave him one of her disgusted looks that said a New Yorker would have been in a deep trance hours ago, but we hicks weren't even smart enough to go under.

So she started over with the "You're getting slee-e-e-e-py," and she went on for about five minutes, which is a long time when you're bored stiff. Then finally she said, "Repeat after me: 'I am in a blissful state.'"

"I am in a blissful state."

It wasn't Luis. Ernie sat there, his eyes closed, his chin on his chest.

"You hypnotized the wrong guy," said Luis.

"Make him bark like a dog!" begged Tuba Dave.

"He's just faking it!" I exploded. "Come on, Ernie, the joke's over."

"The joke's over," Ernie chanted after me.

"This is fresh!" raved Kristy. "Okay, listen, Ernie: You are a better hitter than Babe Ruth."

We all laughed, and Ernie woke up.

"How do you feel?" Kristy asked intently.

"Hungry," said Ernie. "Anybody got a Baby Ruth?"

"Luis, man, you're not relaxed enough," Kristy decided, "which means you've got to concentrate on not concentrating. You dig?"

Luis looked worried and tried to watch the film canister as it swung back and forth.

I was burning inside. Bad enough we were the worst team on the planet; now we were going to get no warm-up, and no batting practice, and all because Professor Pendergast had a granddaughter from New York!

"You're getting sle-e-e-e-py — very sle-e-e-e-py — " she continued in her mystical voice. "Sleepy — and sleepy — and ple-e-ease hurry up and get hypnotized before my arm falls off — ve-e-e-ery sle-e-e-py — "

I was about to stop her when Tim whispered, "Look — he's asleep."

And sure enough, there was Luis, out like a light.

"How do we know he isn't faking?" asked Ernie.

"Simple," said Kristy. She hovered over Luis's ear and whispered. "Luis's mom has stegasaurus breath."

Tim nodded, wide-eyed. "He's hypnotized for real all right," he said positively. "Nobody could just lie there and listen to dinosaur jokes about his mother!"

"Okay, Luis, listen up." Kristy continued in her normal voice. "You're not afraid of the baseball. You're a great catcher, and nothing can hurt you."

"Nothing can hurt me," Luis repeated.

"Now, when I snap my fingers, you're going to wake up. You won't remember any of this, except how grateful you are to your good friend Kristy from New York."

"From New York," echoed Luis.

Then she snapped her fingers, and Luis opened his eyes. "I'm sorry," he said. "I guess I'm just not the type who can be hypnotized."

"But you *were*!" I blurted. And that rotten Kristy belted me right in the ribs.

"Oh, that's okay," she grinned, winking at everybody. "Win some, lose some." She turned to the rest of us. "Come on, dudes! You're missing batting practice!"

We came out of the clubhouse, and there was Mr. Rudolph, the umpire, fast asleep on our dugout steps.

"Oh, no!" exclaimed Ernie. "You don't think he heard us, and now we're going to get thrown out of the League!?"

"What?!" snorted Tuba Dave. "You think there's

a Little League rule that says 'No Hypnotizing?' "

"Wait a minute," Kevin began slowly. "If he was eavesdropping on us, and he heard us hypnotizing Luis, maybe he accidentally got hypnotized, too."

I turned to Kristy. "Can that happen?"

In return I got a diabolical grin that stretched from ear to ear. She leaned close to Mr. Rudolph. "Okay, Ump, this is the way it is: Everything Kevin throws is a strike; everything the other guys throw is a ball. Got that? Okay, when I snap my fingers — "

"You can't do that!" I exploded. "It's not honest!"

"Big talk from last place!" sneered Kristy. She turned back to the umpire. "You won't remember a word of this — "

"Don't listen to her, Mr. Rudolph!" I interrupted. "Call a fair game — "

"Ignore this Goody Two-Shoes!" Kristy urged. "The Tigers are the greatest; everybody else is a bunch of bums!"

"You can't show any favoritism!" I insisted. "Everyone has to have an equal chance — " I fell silent. Mr. Rudolph was awake and glaring at me.

"Johnson, are you saying I'm not a fair umpire?"

He hadn't been hypnotized! He was just having a nap!

"Uh — no, sir. I — uh — just — " I looked around. Kristy was nowhere in sight.

"I never show favoritism!" Mr. Rudolph roared.

"I call 'em as I see 'em, and what I see now is a smart-mouthed kid trying to influence my officiating!"

Professor Pendergast arrived. "What seems to be the trouble?"

"Oh, Grandpa," said Kristy in her best Little Princess voice. "Corey insulted the umpire!"

I had to make a formal apology. I choked it out through my reality sandwich.

But I had to hand it to Kristy. Luis was okay! We got killed, of course, 8–1, but Luis was solid as granite behind the plate. He never even flinched. Maybe there *was* something to this hypnotisim mumbo jumbo.

"Hey, Luis!" I ran up to him after the other team had finished their celebrating. "Sorry about yesterday. And, wow! You were great!"

"Thanks." He looked at me intently. "But my mom *definitely* doesn't have stegasaurus breath!"

"What?" He was *under* when Kristy had told him that! There was no way he could remember it! Unless — "You weren't hypnotized, were you! You faked the whole thing!"

Luis looked faintly embarrassed. "All you guys wanted it to happen so much. And that Kristy — well, she has The Picture, and she just doesn't take no for an answer — "

"She won't be around forever," I predicted with a wink.

"Well," Luis went on, "I just figured if you were willing to go to all that hassle to cure me, I owed it to the team to get cured, even if it was kind of lying."

"And the next time Kevin pitched to you you wouldn't let yourself get scared?" I asked.

"Well, not exactly." He looked embarrassed. "I think I really got cured when you threw that baseball at Tim's brother."

I grinned. "You saw that it didn't kill him, and you felt okay?"

"No way! A great big tough guy like that can take way more pain than me! But when he smashed you right in the face, I thought, How much worse could a little baseball be?"

On cue, my eye throbbed. I didn't mind the pain. My black eye had helped the Feather-Soft Tigers.

"Yo, Johnson!" was Kristy's parting shot. "Don't think I won't remember who cost us this game. We had the ump totally hypnotized until you stuck your nose in, with your small-town-fair-play-nice-guy wimporama!"

I thought of Mr. Lopez, who might have been reading my letter at that very moment.

It wouldn't be long now.

CHAPTER ◇3◇

Second Base — Tuba Dave Jablonski

Tuba Dave Jablonski was a great hitter who never got a hit. No pitcher could get a ball behind Tuba Dave. To us he was King of the Line Drive. To the other teams he was "Easy out! Easy Out!"

The problem was that Tuba Dave, who swung a bat like Ty Cobb, ran bases like Ty Cobb's grandmother. He would smack the ball clear to the outfield and still not give himself enough time to waddle to first base before the throw. And since he only hit *line drives,* he never had the height or the distance for a home run.

Talk about depressing! Here was Tuba Dave, hammering pitches that would have been doubles and triples for any of the rest of us — and the poor guy never even got on base.

"He's totally uncool!" Kristy had the gall to say

over the phone. "He's *so close* to being a star, but instead he's the crummiest player in the league! That's like having the biggest, hypest, most delicious quadruple chocolate cake, but you can't eat it because you know somebody spit in the pan!"

"He's a great hitter!" I said defensively. "He just needs a little more practice base running — "

"More practice isn't going to help!" she cut me off. "Less Tuba Dave is going to help."

"Lay off!" I exploded. "So he's big. So what? He plays tuba in our marching band. Ever lift a tuba? Ever try to march with it?"

Kristy dismissed this with a snort. "My main man P.P. isn't coaching the marching band. Unfortunately, he's stuck with you losers. Which is why Tuba Dave is going on a crash diet starting tomorrow!"

I was torn. Part of me cried out that this was none of Kristy's business. On the other hand, this could help the team! I did stick up for Tuba Dave a little, though. "Listen," I cautioned her. "A guy's weight — that's a totally personal thing. You've got to be careful not to humiliate him in front of the whole team."

She sounded wounded. "Yo, would I hurt a guy's feelings?"

I arrived at practice the next day to find the dugout jammed full of diet booklets. There was the

Scarsdale Diet, the *Prune Juice and Banana Diet,* the *Manchurian Bush Diet, Stir-Fry Your Way to a Brand-New You, Eggplant Extravaganza, Tummy Trimmer,* and a diet that I found just plain scary: *Starving: No Food, No Fat.*

I turned on Kristy in horror. "I thought we agreed not to embarrass the guy! Get these out of here — "

In response, she flashed a dazzling smile, not at me, but at Tuba Dave, who had just walked in. He tossed his glove to the bench and stared at the library of diet literature littering our dugout.

"It's not what you think," I began, but Tuba Dave looked at me, and I could tell he was hurt.

"You know I've been trying to slim down," he said.

I nodded, hating myself.

Tuba Dave picked up a printed brochure that blazoned: *Help at Last with Your Eating Problem.* "I don't have an eating problem," he told us. "I eat great."

"Sure you do!" blurted Ernie. "I mean — not that great! You know — just great enough!"

We all joined in a babbling chorus of approval for the way Tuba Dave ate. All except Kristy. She placed a bathroom scale on the dugout floor. "Okay, Slick," she told Tuba Dave. "Weigh in."

Tuba Dave folded his arms in front of him. "No."

Casually, Kristy jiggled the film canister, which she now wore on a string around her neck.

Totally defeated, Tuba Dave stepped onto the pad. "A hundred and seventy-six pounds?!" He turned accusing eyes on Kristy. "That's impossible! The scale must be broken!"

But Kristy had gathered up the diet booklets, and held them, fanned out like a deck of cards. "Choose your weapon, bro'."

"Aw!" Like a condemned man, Tuba Dave reached over and pulled out the smallest of the brochures. He gaped in horror:

Discover the Diet Secret of Ancient Greece! Delicious HORTA, stewed crabgrass from the Peloponnesus.

"Look at it as an adventure, bro'," Kristy advised. "Check it out. Greek food from the land of the Parthenon, Mount Olympus — "

"Yeah, but *crabgrass*?" cried Tuba Dave, looking very pale.

"Horta," Kristy amended. "Very cool. You picked the best one."

It was too much for our second baseman. He ran off at top speed (about as fast as a quick walk for the rest of us).

"Oh, well," I said to Kristy. "You're not the first person to bomb out at putting Tuba Dave on a diet."

"Too bad," she commented mildly. "He's going to look pretty flabby on eight hundred lockers."

We caught up with Tuba Dave in the parking lot.

"You've got to do it!" begged Ernie.

"Not in a billion centuries!"

"But she's going to develop The Picture!" wailed Tim.

"Let her!"

"What?" Ernie was horrified.

"I was way in the back!" said our second baseman. "Maybe you can't even see me!"

Ernie turned on Kevin. "It's all your fault!"

Kevin stared. "*My* fault?"

"If your dad had gotten our stupid uniforms ready on time, there wouldn't *be* a Picture!"

"Time out!" I shouted, signaling the T. "Just play along with the diet," I told Tuba Dave. "It'll only be for a few days." I dropped my voice to a whisper. "Kristy'll be off our backs pretty soon."

Tuba Dave looked bewildered. "How do you figure that?"

"I wrote a letter to the league president."

"You're a genius," cried Ernie.

"Shhh!" I hissed. "I didn't sign it. She must *never know* it was one of us, or she'll develop the you-know-what!"

Tuba Dave grimaced. "All right, I'll do it. But it better be only a few days."

As it turned out, you couldn't get crabgrass just anywhere. I mean, there was plenty of crabgrass around, just not the right kind that goes into authentic Greek *horta*. We went to nine stores before we found the perfect mixture of grass, dandelion greens, and clover for the recipe. We reported to the Jablonski house just in time to spoil Tuba Dave's dinner.

Mrs. Jablonski had made this great meal with roast chicken and mashed potatoes — *my* mouth was watering, so you can imagine how Tuba Dave felt. The family was around the table. Pieces of chicken were being piled up on his plate. And suddenly, there was Kristy, lecturing his parents about how Tuba Dave was on a new diet, from now on this was all he could eat, and wasn't it wonderful?

I couldn't wait for the Jablonskis to boot her out of the house. But Tuba Dave's parents had been pushing him for a diet for years, so they thought this was a great idea. In fact, Mrs. Jablonski put her own dinner on hold to help Kristy stew up the first batch of *horta*.

"Hang in there," I said to Tuba Dave.

He nodded miserably. "I was sort of hoping the store would be all out, and they'd have to send away to Greece. By boat."

I won't try to build any suspense — the stuff was *disgusting*! We all tried it except for Tuba Dave's little sister, and she was the smart one. I don't much like broccoli and cauliflower, but I have to admit that *horta* was in a class by itself. Long blades of wet grass in a tasteless, watery clump. Unbelievable! Even the adults took a few bites, proclaimed, "Interesting," and turned their attention to the chicken. Tuba Dave only managed a third of a bowl — and I know for a fact he was starving!

As soon as we got out of there, Kristy rubbed her hands together with glee. "He's going to lose weight even faster than I thought! Did you taste that stuff? I'd rather eat garbage!"

"What a terrible diet!" I agreed.

"Are you kidding?" she chortled. "It's the greatest diet in the world, bro'. It's money in the bank. Tuba Dave's going to be burning up the base paths in a couple of weeks!"

I felt a twinge of guilt. Sure, Kristy *was* awful, but she was A-one right that Tuba Dave needed this diet. I actually found myself toying with the hope that Mr. Lopez would take a while before coming to our rescue so Tuba Dave could get thin. It meant more time with Kristy, but that was a small price to pay for making a hitter out of our second baseman.

Kristy put Tuba Dave on daily weigh-ins. By the next practice, he'd *gained* a pound. By our next game, he was up to one-seventy-nine. We lost big, with our expanding second baseman smacking three should-be hits, and never once getting near first base.

Mrs. Jablonski said Tuba Dave was eating his *horta* three times a day, no snacks, no cheating.

Kristy was unconvinced. "No one gains weight eating crabgrass. He must be backsliding. We'll have to watch him."

And when she said "we," she meant *everybody*. She divvied up Tuba Dave's life into time slots and handed them out. I went over to hang around the guy every morning. Tim and Ernie switched off on the afternoons. Different combinations of the three of us and Kristy made sure Tuba Dave was never alone in the evening. When we couldn't keep up the pace, Kevin and Luis helped out. Mrs. Jablonski reported on mealtimes. And Tuba Dave's kid sister was our spy for late night and early morning.

"He's still eating that gross green stuff," Annie Jablonski whispered out her bedroom window to Kristy and me, hiding in the bushes below. "The only other thing he puts in his mouth is that stupid tuba."

From down the hall, we could hear the oompah-pah of Tuba Dave practicing.

"Dessert report," continued Kristy, all business.

"Just us," shrugged Annie. "David hasn't touched a thing."

"Make sure," Kristy ordered. "Weigh all the chocolate in the house, and subtract what you and your folks eat. Then, if the numbers don't match, we nail his butt to the wall."

"How's he been otherwise?" I asked anxiously. "All this diet stuff must be getting him down."

"He's been kind of normal," said Annie. "He talks about the Tigers all the time. Oh, yeah, he's been practicing his music a whole lot. He seems pretty happy."

"Aha!" Kristy snapped her fingers triumphantly. "That proves he's been cheating. Nobody could be happy on a diet of green slime three times a day! This dude should be nasty and rotten and evil! He should make Genghis Khan look like Mr. Rogers!" The oompah-pahs reached us once more. "Instead he's playing a *tuba*! Man, all this practice isn't even helping! Listen to that! It sounds like he's strangling a walrus!"

"Hey!" I interjected angrily. Tuba Dave was a great tuba player, but tonight I had to admit Kristy was right. Our second baseman really wasn't his powerful booming self on the instrument. The sound was weaker — and kind of warbly. "Maybe eating crabgrass messes up your tuba playing. That would explain the extra practicing."

"Something stinks here." Kristy folded her arms in front of her. "I mean, something besides the *horta*."

"Well, I hope it goes on forever," said Annie positively. "David's being extra nice to me, taking out the garbage for Dad, doing all the shopping for Mom — "

"That's it!" cried Kristy.

"Pipe down!" I hissed.

"Don't you get it?" she insisted. "Tuba Dave's doing the shopping! He's buying extra stuff for himself!" She surveyed the house and backyard. "He's got a stockpile hidden around here somewhere, Annie. He's figured out you're watching him, so he waits for you to fall asleep, and then it's major chowtime." She regarded the nine-year-old intently. "When is it safe to search the place?"

"Wait a second!" Now, this was going too far, even for Kristy. "It's one thing to put the guy on a diet and slap him with around-the-clock surveillance. It's something else to break in and search his house. That's illegal!"

"We won't be breaking in," Kristy explained. "Annie will be letting us in. Right, Annie?"

Tuba Dave's little sister smiled conspiratorially. "He's got a tuba lesson at ten tomorrow. He never misses it."

Kristy clapped her hands together with determination. "He's toast!"

◇

We scoured Tuba Dave's closet. We riffled through his underwear. We even took down the guy's light fixture to make sure there was no food up there. Nothing.

But Kristy wasn't done yet. She must have had CIA training. We went through the Jablonski house with a fine-tooth comb. I doubt Tuba Dave would be storing food in his father's golf bag, but that didn't stop Kristy. She checked bookcases for sandwiches jammed behind *Encyclopaedia Britannica*. She opened up the furnace filter! The cedar chest! Mr. Jablonski's toolbox! Then she started opening air ducts!

"Okay," she conceded finally. "No food in here. He must be hiding it outside."

I figured she meant the garage and the garden shed. And yeah, we searched those places. But she also had me beating the bushes and digging holes in the flower beds to look for buried bags of supplies.

"Listen, this is stupid!" I said. "Nobody keeps food outside. The animals would get at it."

Talk to a wall. "If you don't have the guts for this kind of work, Johnson, you shouldn't have signed up for Little League!"

"Forgive me!" I raged. "I didn't read the fine print, where it says you have to have detective skills!"

"Wimp City!" She pointed to the giant oak tree that dominates the Jablonski's backyard. "Okay, up you go."

I stared at her. "The guy can't even waddle to first base. How do you figure he's got a smorgasbord twenty feet straight up?"

She shrugged her famous New York shrug. "If I was eating nothing but crabgrass, I'd swim through molten lava for half a potato chip. Now, alley-oop!"

"It's your idea, *you* do it!"

She jiggled the film canister around her neck. "I'm the photographer; you're the tree climber!"

We were so close to being rid of her! I couldn't let her develop The Picture over one lousy tree. So I scrambled up the big oak. "Now what?" I called down.

"We search *that*!" She was pointing up directly above me.

What *was* that thing? Curiosity got the better of me, and I began to climb up toward it. It was big enough to be a package of food in a brown knapsack. But how would Tuba Dave get way up there? The tree was starting to groan and shake under *my* weight, and I was half of *him*.

"Status report," called Kristy.

"I can't tell yet." I was close, but the sun was bright, and the sharp contrasts of light and shadow made it difficult to see. And then I hoisted myself up on a high branch and looked.

The suspected food stash was a crow's nest, complete with three baby birds.

I was thrilled. I was going to have the privilege of informing the great Kristy that she had *made a mistake*! I might even use one of her phrases, like "reality sandwich," or "Earth to Kristy." I laughed with the pure joy of it. And that was why I didn't hear the mother crow, swooping down to defend her nest from my "attack."

She was the size of a B-52, and red-hot steaming mad. She made a dive-bombing run on my face. I must have cried out, because Kristy yelled, "What is it? Did you find the food?"

But *I* was the food. The mother bird pecked at my head, flapped in my face, and clawed at my shirt. I had to get out of there, but the only direction was down. I tried to swing away from her, but at that moment, there was a sharp cracking sound, and my branch was no longer attached to the tree.

I was falling feet first right at the fence, but I didn't panic. I could come down on the top rail, cushioning the impact by bending my knees. Then I'd simply hop down to the ground. I bounced off the top of the fence like a superball, my legs springing me high into the air. That's when I looked down and saw blue water instead of green grass. Oh, yeah. The Jablonski's neighbors had a pool.

If I had performed that well in the county fair belly-flop competition last fall, I'd have either won first prize or been split open like a sack of oats. The water broke my fall, along with my stomach, in a giant tidal wave splash.

Kristy fished me out using the bug dipper and pried the broken branch out of my hands. "You're wasting your time playing baseball," she commented blandly. "You've got a great future as a daredevil. Captain Gravity, man!"

"There was a crow up there!" I quavered.

"You got off easy." She shrugged. "If that had been a New York crow, it would have had your head off and been stuffing eggs down your neck."

What a great comfort it was to know things could have been even worse.

◇

Get this: At our next practice, Tuba Dave weighed in at a hundred and eighty-one, *up* two more pounds!

Ernie was wide-eyed. *"Crabgrass* is *fattening?"*

Tuba Dave himself shrugged it off. "It's just my nature," he explained. "I'm big-boned."

"If his bones are as big as his butt," Kristy whispered in my ear, "then he borrowed them from a brontosaurus!"

"Shhhh!"

"I've got to give you credit," Tim told the dieter. "That *horta* stuff is so gross! I never thought you'd stick to it."

"Oh, it's all a matter of willpower," Tuba Dave lectured. "And once you get used to it, *horta* isn't all that bad."

Did he really mean that? Or was he just talking big because he knew Kristy was on the way out?

"He's lying his head off, man!" Kristy hissed at me. "And we're going to prove it!"

I was disgusted. "The last time *we* proved something, I almost drowned!" I snarled.

But by then the professor had arrived. I trotted out to left field to shag fly balls, and the subject seemed to be closed.

There was this great old baseball movie on TV. I'd looked forward to it all day. I cleared it with my parents that the set was mine for those two hours. I laid out the pillows so the couch would be just right. I got food and a big bottle of Coke. No sooner were the credits over than Kristy showed up.

"Go away," I told her, not even looking up from the screen.

"No can do, bro'."

"If you won't go away, please shut up. I'm watching a movie."

She stepped right in front of the television. "Tuba Dave is growing, even as we speak."

I was furious. "I don't care if Tuba Dave reaches critical mass! Step aside or die!"

Well, I guess it's pretty obvious by now what the outcome would be. She jiggled her film canister and I ended up going with her. Like common criminals, we went over to Tuba Dave's house and shinnied up the drainpipe into his room. Annie was there to let us in.

"Thanks, kid," said Kristy. "Now, the plan is we hide in the closet, and when he goes for his food stash, we nail him."

"Wait a minute!" I exploded. "It's only nine

o'clock! When's he going to go to bed?"

"He won't be up for a while yet," said Annie. "He's watching this old baseball story on TV, and he loves it. He says it's the best movie he's ever seen."

We hid in the closet. That is, *I* hid in the closet. Kristy made herself at home. She stretched out on the bed, leafing through Tuba Dave's comic book collection; she fooled with his computer, played a few games, and erased half his hard disk by accident; then she pulled on a pair of his jeans, just to show that she could fit a truck in there with her.

"Get in here!" I hissed. "The movie's almost over!" I could tell, because the Jablonskis were applauding downstairs. I had missed the greatest movie in the world. I *dreamed* about the day Mr. Lopez would come to banish Kristy from my life.

She really took her time putting away Tuba Dave's rock polishing kit and joining me in the closet. I was having a fit, because there were already heavy footsteps coming up the stairs.

She flashed me a dazzling smile. "You worry too much, bro'."

I shut the door a split second before Tuba Dave came into the room. I found this next part a little hard to believe. Here it was, eleven o'clock at night, but was Tuba Dave getting ready to go to sleep? No. He pulled his big brass tuba out from under the bed, inserted himself into it, and began to oompah loudly. Kristy and I watched through the crack in the door. He was blowing his brains out — *at this hour*! And the weirdest part was how really bad he was, and getting worse all the time. I remember school concerts where he was the star of the band, blasting clear and true over all the other instruments. Now here he was, puffing and warbling and wheezing and choking! His face was bright blue — he looked like he was suffocating!

Kristy covered her ears. "Man, I'm no tuba expert, but this is toiletsville!" she whispered.

Listening to bad tuba playing is not my favorite thing. And Kristy Pendergast drove me nuts anyway, so being shut in a closet with her was special torture. I couldn't stand another second.

"That's it!" I hissed in a fury. "I'm leaving!"

Kristy grabbed my arm. "What are you — nuts? He'll see you!"

He could hardly miss. I'd be walking out of his closet. "This has gone on long enough!" I said determinedly. "The guy's not cheating! He's eating his crabgrass! The diet doesn't work!"

"He's backsliding!" she insisted. "I'm positive!"

"Let *go*!" I ripped my arm from her grasp, but she just grabbed me around the midsection and held on. But I was determined to get out of there. I mustered my strength for one giant surge, and that was when Kristy let go. I came out of that closet like I'd been shot from a cannon, busting the door clean off its hinges. I caromed right into Tuba Dave.

55

The three of us — me, him, and the tuba — went flying. The crash shook the foundations of the house.

The tuba skittered across the carpet, and out of the bell poured a truckload of M&M's. Billions of them, a universe of candy, a technicolor oompah.

I was thunderstruck. I'd never seen so much chocolate in my life. I didn't know there *was* this much chocolate! The M&M's factory must have been empty!

Kristy bounded onto the scene. A " 'Tsup?" died on her lips as she looked at the sea of multicolored candies.

"I can explain," Tuba Dave began weakly. But the explanation was all too obvious. Tuba Dave hadn't been sticking to his diet at all. He'd been sucking hundreds — no, *thousands* — of M&M's through the mouthpiece of his tuba! No wonder the instrument didn't sound right! He was using it as a giant chocolate straw!

Kristy found her voice again. "You're busted, mister! Who do you think you are — Willy Wonka?"

"It was just a little snack," whined Tuba Dave.

"Little!?" I repeated. "There must be five million calories lying right under our feet! There isn't this much candy in Spooner! How did you get it all?"

Our second baseman hung his head in shame. "I ordered direct from the factory. I told them I was a supermarket chain." He gestured to the floor. "This was meant for Oklahoma."

Then Kristy launched into this long speech about loyalty, honesty, team spirit, respect for the professor, and self-sacrifice. She talked as though, if Tuba Dave didn't stick to his diet, he might as well be selling vital U.S. defense secrets to the enemy.

"So you see why this is so important," she finished, popping a handful of M&M's into her mouth. "Mmmm, these are great."

"Yeah, they sure are," Tuba Dave agreed hopefully and snatched a handful. They never got to his mouth. Kristy grabbed his wrist, and shook until the fingers opened and the candies fell out. Then she took the pillow from his bed, pulled off the pillowcase, and began filling it with M&M's from the floor.

"Come on, Johnson," she ordered. "We're confiscating these on behalf of the Feather-Soft Tigers."

What could I do? I grabbed a handful and joined in.

Two days later, Annie Jablonski reported that her brother never smiled, was mean to her all day long, and was picking constant fights with their parents.

"How about his music?" Kristy inquired.

"His tuba's in the shop," she replied. "He blew

up yesterday and threw it in the neighbors' pool."

I know how the tuba must have felt.

"He's turned into a monster!" she exclaimed. "Every time Mom brings him his *horta,* I want to hide under the table! I'm afraid he's going to go berserk and kill us all!"

It made Kristy glow with pride. "He's following his diet."

But to Tuba Dave, Public Enemy Number One wasn't his mother, or his sister, or even Kristy. It was me.

"*You lied!* She's not gone! She's still here! And I'm gonna *starve*!"

I guess I felt a little guilty. And for the first time another thought crossed my mind: Where was Mr. Lopez?

CHAPTER 4

First Base — Ernie MacIntosh

Around the same time that Tuba Dave went on his diet for real, summer school started. Our first baseman, Ernie MacIntosh, was on the roster as always. Last year it had been for geography. The year before that, Spanish. This time it was one of the biggies. Good old Ernie had flunked math.

"So Mom says I have to miss all our morning practices to go to school," Ernie informed us, his distaste apparent.

"No big deal," said Kristy. "Cut school."

"Okay," shrugged Ernie, and that seemed to be the end of it.

"Wait a second!" I interjected. "What happens when you flunk again?"

"Oh, yeah!" exclaimed Ernie in sudden realization. "There's a pretest to decide if you need to stay in class for the whole summer. If I flunk it, Mom says I have to quit the team!"

"What?" shrieked Kristy. " 'Tsupwitchoor mom, dude? Is she nuts? Didn't you tell her we've only got nine guys and we even stink with *them*?"

"She just said my education is more important than — "

"Yeah, yeah, yeah. We've all heard the lecture. Man, this is *wack*!"

"Wack?" I repeated.

Kristy tried again. "You know — bogus! Toilets-ville! Nonhype! Unchill!" She threw her hands up in exasperation. *"Bad!"*

"Maybe you could study really hard — " Tim began.

"It's not that," Ernie explained. "I get the math right, but the numbers wrong."

"But the math and the numbers are the same thing!" Kristy said reasonably.

I stuck up for Ernie. "I was in his class last year. We studied together." I shrugged. "I can't explain it. He knows how to do everything, but when it comes to the test, he gets all the wrong answers."

Ernie looked sheepish. "It's just that — well, I guess I'm not that smart — "

"Starting today," said Kristy with authority, "you're smart."

"What are you talking about?" I asked suspiciously.

60

"You've got just as much brains as the next idiot," Kristy praised our first baseman. "You don't pass because nobody ever really put the screws to you. Check it out. If you flunk that pretest, I'm not just going to develop The Picture for every locker in the junior high. I'm also going to blow it up to poster size and hang it in the mall, and send a copy to your mother, both your grandmothers, and all your aunts!" And with that, she walked away.

I followed. "What are you, crazy? How can you do this to the poor guy?"

She looked me squarely in the eye. "By the time it's all over, he'll thank me."

When I got back to the dugout, no one was thanking Kristy. A council of war was in progress.

"Remember," Tim was saying. "If she prints up that picture, our lives are ruined for three years of junior high!"

"Longer, even!" Tuba Dave lamented. "In high school it's the same people. We can only hope they forget — "

"They won't," interrupted Ernie. "My great-grandfather wet his pants in kindergarten, and they *still* bug him about it at Spooner Retirement Lodge!"

Kevin snapped his fingers. "I heard about that. Our neighbor's great uncle was in the same class."

"Think about it," Tim went on. "The jokes, the gags — "

The wedgies!" Ernie exclaimed.

"We won't get dates for the senior prom!" added Luis.

Ernie looked at me reproachfully. "I thought you complained to the League president."

I shrugged. "I guess Mr. Lopez is a really busy guy. He'll get around to us."

"But if he doesn't show up before I flunk the pretest, she'll develop the picture!" Ernie wailed.

Tim spoke up. "*If* she has the film. There are nine of us and only one of her."

"We can't beat up a girl!" I argued. "Even if she *is* from New York!"

"We don't have to beat her up," Tim reasoned. "Two of us'll grab her. Somebody opens the canister, exposes the film, and our problems are over."

"The professor's going to be late today," added Kevin. "We'll never have another chance."

I thought it over. We weren't going to *hurt* her — just expose that film. Kristy definitely had it coming after the way she tried to blackmail us and push us around. Look at what Tuba Dave was going through! And me! My black eye was the result of Kristy's "brilliant" plan to help Luis.

"Let's do it."

Kristy was standing out by the mound, wearing her New York bored look — like if invaders from outer space were having a barbecue in center field, she wouldn't bother turning around to watch.

We approached from the rear.

I called out, "Hey, Kristy," and when she turned around, Tim and Ernie grabbed an arm each, and Tuba Dave went for the film. She sweep-kicked Tuba Dave's feet out from under him, and pushed Tim backwards over him. Bobby Ray came forward, but Kristy used her free hand to pull his jersey over his head, blinding him. He blundered right into Ryan. Then she flipped Ernie off her right shoulder, sending him crashing to the ground at the feet of Casper and Luis, knocking them down like bowling pins. At the same moment, she pulled off Kevin's glasses and stuck them on my face! Neither of us could see! We both tripped — him on Casper and me on Tuba Dave. By the time I got those glasses off my nose, the nine of us lay in a heap, and Kristy was lazing on the pitcher's mound like she didn't have a care in the world.

It was totally humiliating. Picture it — nine guys, beaten to a pulp by a girl who didn't really even fight. Just a push here and a trip there.

"Please don't tell the professor," I gasped.

She smiled at us. "I'm proud of you guys. You've got guts."

Yeah. They were scattered all over the grass.

◇

The next day, Ernie sprinted all the way from summer school to the ballpark to show us his practice quiz. He got 14 out of 30. The poor guy was so hopeless at math he didn't even know he was flunking.

"What's this? You're having problems with mathematics?" said Professor Pendergast. "I'd be happy to help you with it."

Of course! You have to know *tons* of math to be a physicist! Here we were with an actual genius as our coach, and nobody even thought of asking him to work with Ernie.

"Gee, that'd be great!" Ernie exclaimed. "How about right after practice?"

"Excellent," approved the professor. "We'll have the house to ourselves. Kristy has gone swimming this afternoon."

That got a big cheer. A whole practice without the little princess!

Our coach was all choked up. "It's wonderful to see she has such good friends."

What?! "Oh, yes!" I managed, crossing my fingers behind my back.

The practice began with new signals for bunt, steal, and hit-and-run, which was kind of stupid because we hardly ever got on base. So my mind was wandering, and that's when it hit me.

"She's *swimming*!" I hissed at Tim.

"Too bad there aren't any great white sharks at the pool," Tim whispered back.

"That's cruel," was Tuba Dave's opinion. "What

did a great white shark ever do to you?"

"Listen," I insisted. "You can't take a roll of film under water, right?"

"So the canister must be just sitting there at the professor's house!" Tim finished excitedly.

We zoomed through our workout in record time. Then I rode back with Professor Pendergast and Ernie. We explained that I was helping Ernie as well.

"Oh, by the way," I added, as though it had just dawned on me. "Kristy has a picture of ours — kind of a team portrait. But we forgot to pick up the film."

The professor directed me upstairs to the guest room. "I'm sure she won't mind. It's the second door on the left."

It was all I could do not to whoop with victory as I sprinted up the stairs and into the room. My jaw dropped. The walls were completely plastered with posters of New York City — the World Trade Center, Empire State Building, United Nations. I looked up. Four different views of the Statue of Liberty gazed down at me.

Then I saw the film canister on the dresser. I nearly wept with joy. No more getting pushed around. No more threats of public humiliation. We were free!

I picked up the canister and pulled off the cap. *Whooooosh!!*

A thick cloud of black smoke exploded out of the

film can right into my face. I began to cough madly.

"Corey, are you all right?" came the professor's voice from downstairs.

"It's just allergies!" I choked out, running to the bathroom. I opened my mouth under the tap and gulped water straight from the sink. That's when I looked in the mirror. My head was caked with gray soot. Desperately, I splashed water in my face. *The stuff didn't come off!* I tried soap. Nothing! Not even when I scrubbed until my cheeks stung!

Heart sinking, I reached inside the canister and pulled out the broken casing of a smoke bomb. On the side was written BIG APPLE NOVELTY CO., NYC.

That rotten Kristy had gotten me again. She had hidden the film and left the smoke bomb in the canister as a booby trap.

I began to panic. What if this guck didn't come off? What if it was permanent?

" 'Tsup!" Kristy rolled in from swimming. She looked at me. "Either a volcano erupted on your face or you found the film can."

"That is the dirtiest, sleaziest, most underhanded thing I've ever seen anybody do!" I seethed.

She laughed. "Glad you liked it."

For her, she was pretty nice. She only busted my chops for about ten minutes before fixing me up. She washed my face with vinegar and the soot came right off. I stank like a salad, but otherwise I was good as new.

We headed downstairs to find Professor Pendergast just as stumped with Ernie as Ernie was stumped with math.

"He understands all of the concepts perfectly," the renowned expert explained, shaking his head. "But he can't seem to arrive at a single correct answer. Most baffling." He raised an eyebrow and sniffed. "Has someone been eating cole slaw?"

Kristy covered up a laughing fit with some coughing. Personally, I didn't find it very funny.

Ernie's pretest was tomorrow afternoon, and things were looking grim for the Toilet Paper Tigers. If the professor couldn't help him, surely nobody could. He would flunk the test, his mom would pull him off the team, and Kristy would develop The Picture. Then we'd all be ruined in Spooner for junior high, probably high school, and maybe even the rest of our lives.

"As I see it, we're up the creek," I told the guys at an emergency meeting before practice. "All we can hope for is a miracle on Ernie's test."

Ryan Crisp spoke up. "There's one thing we haven't tried."

All attention shifted to our right fielder. Ry was always so quiet that if he had an idea, it had to be important.

"Money," said Ry. "New York is the money capital

of the world. Maybe if we offer to *buy* the film — "

"A bribe!" I exclaimed. "It's so sleazy, she'll probably go for it!"

We emptied our pockets. Piggy banks were opened, secret stashes tapped. Allowances were paid in advance. Loans were worked out with brothers and sisters. Annie Jablonski gave Tuba Dave a floating line of credit indexed to the prime rate. He didn't understand it, but he didn't care. We had ten minutes to put our hands on every red cent we could — rolls of nickles, bags of pennies, anything!

Ernie had his summer school books with him so he was elected to be the accountant, since he was the only one with any paper.

"Seventy-six dollars and eleven cents," he reported.

"What?" I squawked. "It's got to be more than that!"

I peered over Ernie's shoulder as he added the long column of figures. ". . . fifteen . . . twenty-three, plus eight makes thirty-one carry the three, two plus three is six, plus nine — "

"Wait a minute," I interrupted. "Two plus three is *five*. Two *times* three is six."

Ernie was wide-eyed. "It *is*?"

The other Tigers cracked up, and started razzing Ernie. But I thought back to Ernie complaining about getting the math right and the numbers wrong. 2×3 and $2 + 3$ probably come into just about every single math question there is. If you had them mixed up, it didn't matter how smart you were — you'd *always* get the wrong answer!

But how could a genius like Professor Pendergast miss something so easy? The answer was simple. The professor was so smart himself — in a million years he'd never think that someone might make a mistake like two plus three equals six.

"Take your money back," I commanded the others. "We're getting an A on that test."

$$2 + 3 = 5 \qquad 2 \times 3 = 6$$

He wrote it two hundred times in his notebook. He chalked it on the dugout wall. It was everywhere — the tops of his sneakers, the bottom of his jersey. We quizzed him all through the practice. As we ran by first base we'd yell out, "Two times three!" and Ernie would have to give the answer. That night, Tim, Tuba Dave, and I tag-teamed a marathon study session at Ernie's. Kristy came by and we wouldn't let her into the house. It was beautiful!

Game day was also pretest day, so Ernie was a wreck. When I stepped up to the plate for batting practice, $2 + 3 = 5 \quad 2 \times 3 = 6 \quad 2 + 3 = 5$ $2 \times 3 = 6$ was printed all the way down the length of my Louisville slugger.

It had been a big morning at the particle accelerator and Professor Pendergast was celebrating like a teenager. The big event: Two leptons had smashed into each other, creating this thing called an antilepton that had lasted for — get this — a *trillionth* of a second. I guess people impress easily in the scientific community.

Tim was having the same thoughts. "He should get a Nintendo or something."

Kristy returned from releasing a large collection of insects into the opposing dugout.

"If you get caught, we could have to forfeit the game!" I hissed.

She shrugged it off. "How many games have you won so far?"

But then I got a hit, and Tim got a hit, and Tuba Dave crunched the ball into the outfield. He never made it to first, of course, but Tim and I both scored. 2–0 Tigers. Our very first lead.

"Is this good? This is good isn't it?" cried the professor, as the rest of us jumped up and down, cheering ourselves hoarse.

Their pitcher was pretty bad, but then Kevin took the mound to show everybody the true meaning of stink. He threw twenty-four straight balls, walking the first six batters. Tie score, 2–2.

" 'Tsupwitchoo?" Kristy stormed the mound. "See that flat thing on the ground in front of Luis? It's called the plate! The ball goes over it! Dig?"

He must've dug, because he floated one over the plate an orangutan couldn't miss. The batter murdered it for a grand slam. 6–2 for the DiStefano Plumbing Orioles.

"There goes my no-hitter," complained Kevin as the game was stopped to search for the ball.

"An antilepton! Who'd've believed it?" was the professor's comment.

For the first time ever, we fought back. It was great! I'd swing my bat — and the ball would actually be there! I got a single and a double, Luis belted a home run, Ryan and Ernie both got hits. Even Tuba Dave looked a little closer to the bag when they threw him out at first.

We managed a little defense, too, although it was mostly Bobby Ray, who was awesome at shortstop. At the end of the sixth the score was tied 8–8. The Feather-Soft Tigers were going to extra innings.

The professor was so used to losing that he tried to go home. I guess he was pretty anxious to see if the particle accelerator could crank out another antilepton. But when we explained that we might actually *win,* he was so happy he forgot about science. We were pretty hyper ourselves.

"This is what we waited for all winter." Tim grinned.

"What a great game!" agreed Luis.

I didn't say anything because I was watching the Orioles make a pitching change. All of a sudden it hit me. Little League rules said no pitcher could go for longer than six innings. Kevin had to be replaced, too!

I ran across the dugout bellowing, "Professor!"

Kristy put her hands over her ears. "Mellow on the volume control, dude."

I told our coach about the Little League rules.

He looked confused. "How can Kevin *throw out* his arm? It's attached."

"Listen up, dudes," announced Kristy. "Tuba Dave is pitching."

I choked. *"What?* He's not a pitcher! *I'm* a pitcher!"

"That moves Kevin over to second," she finished.

Boy, did I blow my stack! I got in Kristy's face and started screaming, *"It's not fair! You just don't want me to be the pitcher! It's none of your business who's the pitcher! You can't make me not be the pitcher . . ."* And I kept on howling while Caspar struck out, and Ryan and Luis grounded out to end our half of the inning.

I folded my arms in front of me. "I refuse — I absolutely *refuse* — to go along with this!" And I stood my ground while the rest of the players took the field. The problem was that when Mr. Rudolph came and ordered me to take my position, the only open spot was in left field. Well, I couldn't fight with the umpire in the middle of a game. So I went, biting back my rage.

"Play ball!"

Tuba Dave gave up a hit to the leadoff man, but the second Oriole popped straight up to Luis. The next guy hit a dribbling grounder along the first base line. It was an easy double play, which would make three outs. The inning was over!

But there was Ernie, droning over and over, "Two *times* three equals six . . . two *plus* three . . ." He picked up the ball on "three," so he threw it — *to third base*!

The runner was the second most shocked guy in the place. The most was Caspar Howard, our third baseman. Totally bewildered, he tossed it back to Ernie, who stepped on the bag, and the batter was out.

"Excellent!" cheered the professor.

"The *other* guy!" cried Kristy. "Get the other guy!"

They'd forgotten about the lead runner, who was rounding third.

Befuddled by too much studying, Ernie threw to second. By the time Kevin got the ball on its way to Luis, the winning run was halfway home, and nothing could stop him.

Suddenly, out of nowhere, a pink high-top sneaker was on the base path between the runner's feet, and he was tripping, tumbling, sliding in a cloud of East Texas dust. Luis made the tag easily.

"I *saw* that!" Mr. Rudolph ran after Kristy, who

was strolling casually back to our dugout.

"*Tripped* him?" exclaimed Kristy in her best "little princess" voice. "Grandpa, I would *never* do that! Did you see me trip anybody?"

The professor went for it, hook, line, and sinker. I wish I could say the same for Mr. Rudolph. He counted the run, and we lost, 9–8.

◇

The next day, I went to summer school to stand with Ernie when the results of the pretest were handed down. Wouldn't you know it — Kristy was already there.

"He better've passed, after he cost us that game!" she growled.

"I don't remember Ernie getting caught interfering with a base runner," I pointed out coldly.

"It was our only chance, bro', and whose fault was that? What kind of idiot mixes up three, the number, with third, the base?"

Probably the same kind of idiot who thinks two plus three equals six.

Ernie burst out of a classroom like a freight train. "A-minus!" he shrieked with joy, waving his paper in the air. "No more summer school!"

I was thrilled for the guy. I was about to shake his hand when he threw his arms around Kristy and *kissed* her right on the cheek! "Thanks a million!" he said, from the heart.

"Don't sweat it, bro'," she replied. "Anytime."

After she'd left, I turned on our first baseman. "Are you crazy? How can you thank *her*? After what she was going to do to you — to *us*! And she still might do it!"

Ernie shrugged. "If it wasn't for her I'd be off the team. I don't think she's that bad."

And he walked away, leaving me clawing at the walls.

Come on, Mr. Lopez! Hurry!

CHAPTER 5

Right Field — Ryan Crisp

The problem with losing a close one is that you keep going over it in your mind. When you get creamed 20–0, nobody thinks, If that line drive had only drifted foul in the top of the third . . . But when you were tied after six innings, one little break could have made the difference. Who could resist replaying the game over and over? Every called strike, every close tag.

The one that really bugged me came in the bottom of the fifth. One out, nobody on base. The batter hit a long fly ball to right field — directly at Ryan Crisp. It was an easy out, right? Wrong! Our right fielder was asleep! I didn't know it was even possible to sleep standing up if you weren't a horse! The ball came down right on his head. At least it woke him up, but by then the "easy out" had turned into a triple. The next Oriole popped up to me — which would've been three outs if Ry had caught that ball. But no, the inning was still alive, and the runner tagged up and scored. And we lost. Again.

Now, I'm no crybaby, and I realize the rest of us didn't exactly play like stars either. But it was the coach's job to say something to Ry. And since our coach was still celebrating the antilepton, I figured I'd bring up the subject — gently, with tact.

"You know that ball you took in the head?" I began.

Ryan blinked. "Sorry. I lost it in the sun."

"Oh." This was going to be harder than I thought.

"Let me try," said Luis. "Ry, all the other fielders were awake — "

"I've got a new glove," Ry explained. "And the pocket is stiff." I think he expected us to believe that was why a fly ball had bounced off his head.

"Put it this way," Tuba Dave took a stab at it. "You know how some people are into sleepwalking? Well, let's just say there was such a thing as sleep-fielding — "

He was interrupted by a snort of disgust. We wheeled to find Kristy standing there. "Lose the jive, dudes! Cut to the chase! Get to the point," she added for those of us who didn't speak New Yorkese. She turned on Ryan. "You were asleep, man! Crashed out! Catching Z's! A-snooze! Sawing logs! Chilling with the sandman! 'Tsupwitchoo?"

"The ball took a bad hop," Ry offered.

"Yeah," Kristy agreed. "Off a hollow sphere! So let's make sure it doesn't take any more! Go to bed early!"

"I can't," said Ry. "Tonight's the night I stuff envelopes for Merkel's Department Store."

"Well, tomorrow night, then."

Ry shook his head. "Tomorrow I sweep up at the print shop." He looked thoughtful. "And Wednesday I wash dishes at Sal's Diner. And Thursday I'm on envelopes again. And Friday — "

"All right, all right," Kristy interrupted. "I get the picture. How about sleeping late in the morning?"

Ryan shook his head. "Can't. I deliver the *Dallas Morning News*."

Kristy was getting really steamed. "An afternoon nap, then."

"The Spooner paper comes out in the afternoon," Ry explained.

She was tearing her hair. "You deliver that, too?"

He shrugged. "I wanted to pick up a little extra money."

She snapped. "What are you — *General Motors*? Are you listed on the stock exchange? Sure you're not into any other little businesses? Like aerospace? Shipbuilding? Putting out oil well fires?"

Ry scratched his head. "Well — I make deliveries for Mr. Shaughnessy at the drugstore, I walk dogs, I water plants for people who are out of town, I caddy at the country club, cut lawns, and I sometimes baby-sit."

We all stared at him. No wonder he had fallen asleep in right field. I'm amazed he didn't *die* out there! None of us knew Ry Crisp that well, even though he went to school with us. He lived on a farm out of town, so we saw him in class but that was pretty much it. Now we knew why. The guy worked twenty-five hours a day!

"Why don't you stick a broom up your pants?" Kristy suggested. "That way you can sweep the street while you're doing all that stuff! I mean — you're a major corporation, man! How much do you make — the Gross National Product?"

Ryan looked hurt. "I like to do my bit to help out my family," he said with dignity.

It shut up even Kristy. It was easy to picture. A small farm, tough times, struggling parents, and their son — who was working night and day to pull his weight. Who could get mad at a guy like that?

We practiced for a while, but then Ry had to run off to deliver the afternoon paper. Kristy immediately called a meeting. "We've got to do something about Ryan."

"Oh, yeah!" Tuba Dave said bitterly. "He's working to help his parents; he really needs crabgrass!"

"Lay off Ry," I told her. "He's got enough problems."

Kristy rolled her eyes at me. "Would those of us

whose IQ's are *larger* than our shoe sizes please listen up," she said to the others. "Now — how are we going to help Ry?"

"Help him?" I repeated. "How can we make his dad's farm any better? We'd have to control the weather, and the price of corn, and stuff!"

"Paging Doctor Brain!" she sang out. "Look — Ry is the greatest guy in the world for what he's doing. When he was talking about helping out his folks, I had tears in my eyes!"

Luis was thunderstruck. "Cry? *You?*"

"New Yorkers are human, too, you know," said Kristy, insulted. "Just because we're twenty times cooler than everybody else doesn't mean we don't have emotions. So here's my plan."

"Let me guess," I snarled. "You're going to threaten that unless he grows twenty million bushels of corn this year, you'll develop The Picture."

"Oh, that," Kristy said airily. "I already developed it."

There was a gasp as all eight of us sucked in air.

"Well, I had to make room for the smoke bomb," she reasoned.

Ernie's eyes popped. "Not at the mall?"

"Chill out," she advised. "P.P. has a darkroom in the basement. It's a hype hobby, you know."

"You lied to us!" I stormed. "You said if Ernie passed that test — "

"Don't be wimps! Nobody's seen it yet." Her eyes gleamed. "Except me."

We were in agony. When The Picture was just film, it wasn't really a picture — it was the *possibility* of a picture. Now there was a real Picture in the world. It was like living with a ticking time bomb.

"What's it look like?" Tuba Dave barely whispered.

"Oh, very artistic. Brilliant camera angle. You want to hear the plan or not?"

Typical Kristy. Now that she had us over a barrel, she was going to tell us what we had to do. I steeled myself for the most outrageous scheme of all.

"We're going to pitch in and help Ry help his folks," she said with determination.

None of us could believe it. I almost felt guilty for my letter to Mr. Lopez. Here was a noncrazy idea from Kristy! No sneaking around, no hiding, no tree climbing, just plain honest work for a good cause. We help Ryan and his parents, and help the team, too. With a little less work, Ry wouldn't be falling asleep in right field anymore.

Ry was really grateful. "You guys are the best! I can't believe you'd do this for me!"

And there followed several days of the worst

81

slavery known to man. I don't know how Ry managed to do all this by himself, because it was far too much work for the eight of us, *and* Kristy, *and* the professor. Kristy had him making drugstore deliveries in his van.

The paper routes were the worst. With a hundred and fourteen addresses straight up the steepest hill in town, the *Morning News* could take until midnight to deliver! And on Sunday, forget it! The wagon weighed ten thousand pounds! Not to mention boring! When my Walkman batteries ran out, I cried!

"You're lucky," said Luis bitterly. "I baby-sat the Feliciano triplets. They got saxophones for their birthday!"

Ernie held out his hands, which were covered in Band-Aids. "Look at this!"

"Nice manicure!" Kristy guffawed. "What'd you use — a lawnmower?"

"It's paper cuts!" said Ernie indignantly. "I was stuffing envelopes until two o'clock in the morning! And the licking part! Yeccch!"

"I'll do that next," offered Tuba Dave.

"Oh, no you don't," put in Kristy. "The glue is peppermint flavor, and that means calories, Jumbo. You're on caddy duty. That's good exercise."

"Try not to get Father Flanagan," groaned Bobby Ray. "He drove our golf cart into the water hazard and left me there. How does Ryan stand it?"

"He's helping out his folks," Kristy reminded him. "He's a great kid."

"By the way, where *is* Ry?" I asked.

"At home," Kristy replied. "I gave him the day off so he could catch up on his sleep."

On Wednesday, I flipped out. I swallowed my pride, got down on my knees, and begged Kristy to take me off the paper route.

"Okay, but stop groveling," she ordered. "You're making me sick." She began manipulating game pieces on her handmade job board. "If I move Luis to papers — " She switched places between a toy soldier and a size "C" battery, " — that bumps Caspar over to Sal's Diner — "

"Who's the raisin?" I asked.

"That's Kevin. He switches to envelope stuffing."

"Where am I?"

She pointed. "You're the dead cricket."

"Aw, come on!" I exploded. "Why do I have to be a bug? Can't you find a rock or something?"

"We've got a rock. It's Ernie."

I've had stupider conversations, but not many. "What's *your* symbol?" But I could already see it — a silver Statue of Liberty placed over a square marked Control Center. I guess the professor's game piece was a lepton, because I couldn't see it.

With her pen, Kristy pushed the dead cricket over past the Feliciano triplets, across the dairy, round the caddy shack, and over to a red fire hydrant.

I looked at her questioningly. "Ryan's on the fire department, too?"

She laughed in my face. "You're a dog walker. Have a nice day."

◇

Big Al was named after Al Capone, the Chicago gangster. I now know this is a terrible insult to Mr. Capone. Big Al was part St. Bernard, part elephant, and part warthog. He thought he was a person, but he wasn't even a dog. When we walked by, little kids burst into tears. One six-year-old looked at his mom accusingly and said, "You told me the mammoths all died like the dinosaurs!"

They crossed the street to walk on the other side.

Big Al smelled like a wet rug, except for his breath, which was in a category by itself. Squirrels and chipmunks scattered from half a block away. I practiced mouth-breathing.

Big Al weighed two hundred pounds; I weighed ninety. He was taking me for a drag down Main Street, smashing me off mailboxes and trees, when I spotted the professor's van. I called out a greeting: "HE-E-E-E-ELP!"

Kristy's grinning face poked out of the passenger window. " 'Tsup? Hey, what a cute puppy!"

"Sit!" I pleaded. "Heel! Roll over! Play dead! Aw, come on, dog, *stop*!"

The professor parked, and Kristy leaned out the

window and bellowed at the top of her lungs, *"Yo!"*

Big Al stopped in his tracks, which caused me to rear-end him. Then he trotted up to the car and presented his big ugly head to be patted.

"Who's the hypest, freshest canine dude?" Kristy crooned, stroking his fur — no two hairs pointed in the same direction!

Wouldn't you know it? Big Al, who hated every-thing and everybody, including his own tail, which he thought was following him, was a sucker for Kristy Pendergast. She played with his ridiculous ears, rubbed noses, shook hands, traded kisses, and treated him a heck of a lot better than she ever treated me.

Then the professor said, "Come along, Princess. We've got deliveries to make." He started the van and drove off.

It hit me a split second too late that Big Al might not want to lose the one thing he'd ever liked in his miserable, smelly life. His first lunge yanked the leash out of my hands; his second took him a block down the street. I ran like crazy, but in two minutes the van was out of sight, and ten seconds later, so was Big Al.

The police wouldn't take my report.

"I thought you said it was a dog!" exclaimed Officer Collins after I gave the description.

"It *is!*"

"Okay, let's start again. What color?"

"A sort of blackish, brownish, grayish, mustard — "

"Nothing looks like that," said the officer, ripping up the paper. "Get out of here."

I spent the next two-and-a-half hours on my bike, scouring Spooner for Big Al. All I found was Ry. He was just coming out of the movies. It kind of bugged me for a second. Here I was, busting my hump over *his* dog-walking job, while he had fun! Not that I didn't think it was great how his was earning money for his family. But we were supposed to be *helping,* not *doing* it for him!

I gave up and headed for Mr. Cacciatore's place. I was going to have to do the honorable thing, and tell the man I'd lost his beloved pet.

When I arrived, bathed in sweat and limp as a rag, I found Kristy there, playing in the yard with her dear friend Big Al.

"You're late, dude."

I put in my request to go back on the paper routes.

At practice the next day, Ry looked like a million dollars; *I* fell asleep in the outfield. Bobby Ray was allergic to the dishwashing soap at Sal's, so he was one big itch from head to toe. Luis was so stiff from sweeping the print shop that, when he went into his catcher's crouch, he couldn't straighten up again. Kevin had been cutting lawns all week, and was too exhausted to put any zip on his pitches. But that was okay. Except for Ryan, none of us had enough energy to swing at them. Poor Ernie missed the practice altogether. He'd been watering plants, and was now at the doctor's office, having three cactus needles removed from his behind. The professor/drugstore delivery boy was sacked out in the dugout.

When the practice was over, Ry left to go swimming, and I stormed Kristy. "Hey, wait a minute! Isn't he going to stay and help on *some* of his jobs?"

Kristy shrugged. "It's only been a few days. That's not enough time for a full recovery."

"He just blasted the longest home run ever hit in this park! He can *at least* do the afternoon papers!"

"Look," Kristy challenged, "who's running this team, you or me?"

"The *professor*!" I shot back.

As if on cue, a loud juicy snore rumbled out of the dugout.

"Okay, everybody," Kristy called out, "cough up the do-re-mi! Produce the juice! Fork over the *dinero*! Lay out the moola! Bank the bread! Lose the bucks! Pay up," she translated. She held open a Bloomingdale's bag, and we all stuffed in the money we'd made doing Ryan's work.

"I don't see why I should have to pay!" I said

bitterly. "I almost got killed walking Big Al!"

"That's nothing," said Tim feelingly. "I was on plant watering and the Venus flytrap closed on my hand! It was *gross*!"

Tuba Dave stared into the bag. "We've got a fortune here!"

"We could buy Ry a whole new farm!" Ernie added, breathless with wonder.

"Isn't it hype?" grinned Kristy. "It's going to be totally heartwarming to see the Crisps' faces when we hand them all this cash-ola!"

I think she was trying to make us believe she had a heart.

◇

By Saturday, the bag was bursting at the seams with money, and the Feather-Soft Tigers were the best paper boys, dishwashers, envelope stuffers, sweepers, plant waterers, delivery boys, caddies, dog walkers, and baby-sitters in all of Little League, even if we still stank at baseball.

So the professor loaded us into his van for the ride out to the Crisp farm.

Kristy was rubbing her hands together with anticipation. "What a great surprise for Ry!"

"Now, Princess," said Professor Pendergast as we tooled along the highway through flat, open pasture land. "You know money doesn't solve everything."

"I know, Grandpa," said Kristy, "but it's a really good beginning."

"Beginning?!" Ernie was horrified. "You can't mean I have to go back to the Millers' cactus garden?" he asked from atop a stack of soft pillows on the seat.

"Of course not," she replied. "But now the Crisps have a nice little nest egg, and Ry can quit some of his jobs without feeling guilty."

"And since he's taking it easier," Tim added, "he won't be falling asleep in right field."

"It feels terrific to help someone," said Luis. "Right, Corey?"

"Right," I said absently, but I wasn't really paying attention. Where was Ryan's house? We'd passed the sign that said CRISP at least twenty minutes ago. On both sides of the road, there was grazing land as far as the eye could see, and about a zillion head of cattle, mostly longhorns and Brahmas.

"We must've missed it," Kristy decided.

"There haven't been any exits," the professor pointed out.

At that moment, a shiny white car marked RANCH SECURITY flagged us down, and a uniformed man in mirrored sunglasses got out.

"Can I help you folks?"

"We're looking for a small farm — the name is Crisp."

The man laughed as though the professor had just told the most hilarious joke in history. "Straight up the road on the right. You can't miss it."

It *was* straight up the road — thirty miles later — the biggest, most beautiful sprawling ranch house in the universe, dotted with skylights and cedar decks. We stopped on a rise just to look at it, spread out before us. It had a four-car garage, two swimming pools, tennis courts, and riding stables.

I think it hit all of us at the same time. We weren't *on our way* to the Crisp farm; we'd been *there* for the last hour. And all that land, all that cattle, and this Texas mansion belonged to Mr. and Mrs. Crisp, whose son Ry was "helping out" by doing a few odd jobs around Spooner!

"You know those ranches you hear about," said Ernie, "where it takes a day to drive from one end to the other? Well, I think this is one of the bigger ones."

"It's got everything!" breathed Tuba Dave.

"Where's the cemetery?" said Kristy between clenched teeth. "They're going to need one as soon as I get my hands on Ry! Can you believe him — maxin' and relaxin', livin' large on our hard labor?"

"Not The Picture?" gasped Ernie.

But Kristy was already herding us back into the van.

"Come on, Grandpa. I'm really looking forward to giving Ry what he's got coming to him."

We parked in the circular driveway, and the maid directed us out back to the hot tub. There, in solitary splendor, soaked our right fielder.

I was carrying the Bloomingdale's bag. "Are we really going to give this to him?" I whispered. It felt like bringing a tray of ice cubes to an Eskimo.

Kristy grabbed the bag from my hands, and dumped all the money out on Ryan's towel. "Here's the cash we earned so that you and your parents don't have to starve!"

Ryan was taken aback. "I never said we were starving; I just said I was helping them out."

"Well, you did a great job," said Kristy sarcastically. "I'll bet all this was a pile of dirt before you started delivering the *Dallas Morning News*! Well, keep your mitts off *this dinero*! It's going straight to charity! Now, any last requests before I throw a toaster in there and fry you?"

Ryan shrugged. "I thought you knew about our ranch."

I had to speak up. "But all those jobs! Big Al! The paper routes! Why? What do you do with the money?"

In answer, Ryan got out of the water, and led us to a gleaming white structure that had once been a barn. He threw the doors wide.

We gawked. Six Flags didn't have that much stuff. There were pinball machines, arcade games, Skee-ball, juke boxes, Pokerino, Foosball, air hockey, Bowlerama, three holes of miniature golf, fortune-telling machines, prize wheels, Indy 500 — *everything*! Even one of those test-your-strength doohickeys where you hit the thingamajig with a hammer and try to ring the bell.

"I bought it all with my own money," said Ry proudly.

We were blown away, all except Kristy. She had this intense look on her face. I couldn't tell if she was going to strangle Ry, or go play Super Mario Brothers. She walked up to a midway game called Tank Command, and sat down at the tank turret. Then she swung it around and fired a tennis ball with deadly accuracy right at Ryan's chest.

A delighted grin split her face. "Batter up?"

CHAPTER ⟨6⟩

Third Base — Caspar Howard

Here's a confession. I was really glad Mr. Lopez didn't show up that week. If he had, Kristy would have been gone, and we never would have discovered Tank Command. The game shot tennis balls at cardboard cutouts of helicopters and troop carriers, but it was *perfect* for batting practice. We hauled the gun part onto our diamond, and plunked it down in the middle of the outfield. Then we formed a wide circle around it, standing poised with our bats. Wearing Luis's catcher's mask, Kristy would sit at the gun and fire her way around the circle, pitching to us one at a time.

It was amazing! We could all practice at once; the air-powered gun never got a sore arm, and fired the tennis balls faster than any pitcher in the league; and was it ever accurate! Kristy could pitch them high, low, inside, outside — I'm amazed the pros never thought of this! With Tuba Dave looking slimmer every day, and Ry cutting his jobs down to just the print shop and the Felicianos, the Tigers were shaping up into a lean, mean baseball machine.

Except for Caspar Howard.

The professor noticed first. "That boy there — the one playing left base — I don't think he's having fun." I guess left base was lepton language for third, since it was to the left of the plate.

It was true. Caspar didn't look happy, and it had nothing to do with our 0–4 season. He was an okay third baseman, but he played like a zombie. And as a hitter — forget it. You could tell he was just swinging to get his at bat over with. I don't think he'd had a hit all season. Even during Tank Command batting practice, Caspar looked like he was reading the telephone book. If Little League was supposed to be a great experience, it sure wasn't working for Caspar Howard.

"P.P.'s right," said Kristy. " 'Tsup with that guy?"

"It's none of our business," I said hastily.

Wrong. Everything in the known universe was Kristy's business. She pointed at Caspar's sad-sack face. "*That* is like chicken pox. It's contagious. If we don't stop it now, pretty soon the whole team's going to be moping around like a bunch of undertakers with that wack sourpuss frown. Remember, happy dudes hit more home runs."

"You sure made Tuba Dave happy," I said sarcastically.

If you don't agree with Kristy, she pretends you didn't speak at all. "Yo, Caspar!" she called. "Come on over here!" And when he came, she said, "Johnson here wants to have a talk with you, man to man." And she walked away!

"Uh — right," I managed. "So — what's new?"

"Nothing much," Caspar shrugged. "What did you want to talk about?"

I swear — if I could have thought of any other subject, I'd have done it! But you can't just pull a guy off third base and say, "Hey, how about those new doughnuts with the cream in the middle?" And I ended up doing what Kristy wanted. Again. "So, Caspar, what do you think of the Tigers?"

He looked unimpressed. "They're okay, I guess."

"You don't seem to be getting into it," I pointed out.

"Sure I am," he lied. "It's just that I'm not a real big baseball fan."

"Then why did you sign up for Little League?"

Caspar avoided my eyes. "My dad really wanted me to."

I thought back. Mr. Howard had been there for our first couple of games, but not since then. Who could blame him? For a true baseball fan, watching the Tigers would be almost painful. And, let's face it, Caspar *was* kind of the crummiest of the crummy.

"He played baseball in college," our third baseman explained. "He even had a tryout with San Diego. I — " He studied the grass. "I've got other interests."

"Such as?" I prompted. Talk about nosy! Kristy was turning me into a Junior New Yorker!

Caspar avoided my question. "You know, hobbies — personal stuff."

Fair enough. Caspar was doing his best for the Tigers, even though he was into other stuff.

"What other stuff?" Kristy asked after practice.

I shrugged. "He didn't want to talk about it."

She threw her hands up in disbelief. "Way to go, Johnson!" she blamed me. "Now we've got to deal with this problem, and we don't even know the tip!"

"The tip?"

"The scoop! The lowdown! The story! The info! The bottom line! The deal!"

I glared at her. "Sorry. I'll bet in New York Little League everyone can read minds!"

"They can ask a simple question! The reality sandwich makes you sharp, man! Now we have to find out Caspar's hobby."

"Count me out," I told her.

◇

She counted me in. And, worse still, she did it at five o'clock in the morning, with the old rocks against the window trick. But this was Texas in July. The gravel got caught in my window fan. It sounded like a machine gun firing at a helicopter. I peeled myself off the ceiling in time to see my fan short out in a shower of sparks. In the silence that followed, a voice called, "Pssst, Johnson! 'Tsup?"

"If I have to come out there," I hissed, "I'm bringing my father's rifle!"

"Get down here, Johnson!" she rasped. "P.D.Q.!"

"Go back to bed!" I snarled. "That's what I'm doing!"

And then the barrage of pebbles against the broken fan was so loud that I had to get dressed and go downstairs before she woke up my parents. I got out onto the lawn just in time to keep her from launching a hunk of concrete that would have gone through my window, clear down to the basement, and pushed our house halfway to the earth's core.

She grabbed my arm and began hauling me down the street. "Caspar's on the move!"

"It's five o'clock in the morning! Where would he be going?"

She cast me a look of disgust. "If you had *asked*

him yesterday, we wouldn't have to be doing this!"

Oh, so this was *my* fault. That explained it. "How do you know he's up? Were you hiding in his closet?"

"Nah. My main man P.P.'s got this hype telescope. He looks at Jupiter, but it works for Caspar's place, too." She pointed. "There he is!"

We slipped into the shadow of a fence. There was Caspar, a gym bag over his shoulder, walking down the street. Believe me, a predawn stroll with my worst enemy wasn't what I had in mind. But as soon as I saw Caspar, curiosity got the better of me. We followed him past the baseball diamond, past downtown, to the Spooner Public Library and Community Center on Lamar Street. The library was closed, and so was the Community Center, but the ice rink — the only one in town — was open.

"Hockey?" I whispered.

Kristy shook her head. "No stick."

We slipped inside and hid behind the scoreboard. From there we could see the whole ice surface, but nobody could see us. The cold of the arena made me shiver after the muggy air outside.

Caspar laced on a pair of skates and stepped over the boards. In three long strides, he was up to speed. He was a figure skater, and he was great, executing spins, leaps, and unbelievable jumps. I don't know much about figure skating, but Caspar

Howard looked as good as those guys from the Winter Olympics.

I waited for Kristy to fire away at our third baseman with both barrels. He was a wimp, and a sissy, and a ballerina, and a loser, and in a million years no guy from New York would behave like this. Instead, she said, "Do you realize what a great athlete you have to be to do what he's doing?"

On cue, Caspar executed a triple jump that blew me away. "He's fantastic!" I enthused. "Let's go congratulate him!"

She looked at me pityingly. "It's five A.M. — do you know where your brain is? If we show up now, he'll see we've been spying on him, and he'll never trust us again. And then the Tigers lose all that energy that could be channeled toward baseball."

"Toward *baseball?*" I repeated. "I'm not putting down skating, but it's got nothing to do with baseball. Caspar doesn't even *like* baseball. He's only on the team to please his dad."

"An athlete is an athlete," lectured Kristy the great sports expert. "If he can do that" — she indicated the rink — "he can play baseball. He just has to *want* it."

"He'll say no." I told her.

"I'm not planning to *ask.*"

Tuba Dave looked around the field. "No Tank Command?" It was practice the next day, and Ry's carnival game was nowhere in sight.

"Chill out, Babe Ruth," said Kristy. "We're working on our legs today."

"Legs?" repeated Ernie.

There was general grumbling. We all loved Tank Command.

"Legs," said Kristy. "You know — the two skinny things that hold up the rest of you. After all this batting practice, there's a slight chance some of you might get on base. And your base running is toiletsville. So we're putting you to work."

"Running?" asked Luis.

"Skating," she amended.

In the confused murmur that followed, I snuck a look at Caspar. For the first time all summer, he had come to life.

Kristy was annoying, but never let it be said that she wasn't prepared. When the guys all started complaining, she pulled out a diagram of the human leg. The lecture started: The Achilles tendon goes here, and the uvula tenses the muscles around the fibius and, if you don't skate, you may as well chop your legs off. Who could argue with that?

The professor loaded us into the van and took us over to the Community Center. While the others were renting skates, I snuck into the library and pounced on the dictionary. There is no such thing as a fibius, and the uvula is in your mouth. In other words, Kristy was doing it to us again.

Where was Mr. Lopez? It had been *weeks* since he'd gotten my letter. How busy can a guy be? I felt a chill deep in my bones. Last year when I sent away for the "Great Pitchers" sticker album, it took two months to show up. If Mr. Lopez made us wait that long, the season would be over! We'd be insulted, and blackmailed, and pushed around by that obnoxious New Yorker *all summer*! I'd *never* get the chance to pitch!

"Yo, Johnson," came Kristy's voice. "Get your butt in here and score some skates."

In East Texas, if your behind isn't dragging on the ice, you're skating. Most of us had only tried it once or twice in our whole lives. We hated it; and we hated Caspar for being good at it. Even I, who knew in advance about Caspar, kept hoping that the giant Zamboni ice scraper would drive out and flatten him.

We fell down; we ran into each other; we skated on our ankles; when we finally did get going a little bit, the spiked part on the front of the blade would dig in, and we'd go flying. Then Kristy made us try skating backwards. It gave us a whole new side of our heads to smash on the ice when we went down. Caspar started doing jumps and spins. We wanted him dead.

"Come on, dudes!" cheered Kristy. "Exercise those uvulas!"

I grabbed a bunch of guys and we tripped/limped/crawled over to Kristy.

"All right, the joke's over!" I said, making for the gate. "If we hurry, we can still get in a half-practice."

She blocked my way. "Get back out there, Johnson."

I shook my fist, causing me to lose my balance and fall crashing to the ice. Tuba Dave and Tim hauled me up again. "Skating has nothing to do with baseball!" I rasped. "It's a waste of time and everybody hates it! We're leaving *now*!"

She was unimpressed. "Aren't you forgetting my new hobby, *photography*? My main man P.P. says I'm getting really good in that darkroom."

The others backed up and Luis slipped and conked his head, but I stood firm. "I'm not so sure. You said you developed The Picture more than a week ago. So where is it?"

"Don't worry," said Kristy. "It's safe and sound."

"How do we know there even *is* a Picture?" put in Tim.

"Maybe you were lying to us," added Tuba Dave.

In answer, Kristy reached into her pocket and produced an envelope. "It's right in here."

"Big deal, an envelope!" I snorted. "Come on, Kristy, is there a Picture or not?"

The problem with calling Kristy's bluff is that

she's never bluffing. She opened the envelope, and pulled the contents out about a third of the way.

We stared. It was The Picture all right! Only the bottom was showing, but we could still make out a row of bare feet on a concrete floor. Then Kristy snapped the envelope out of view. The other players panicked. They started skating at breakneck speed, falling all over each other.

I scrambled after them. "Come back! We can't let her spook us like this!"

They accelerated. "I'm not messing with her," yelled Tuba Dave. "That's The Picture! The *real* Picture!"

" 'Attaway, dudes!" called Kristy.

At last, the professor stepped forward, bearing hot chocolate for everybody. Never mind that is was ninety-eight degrees outside. Actually, it was fantastic. It tasted like *no more skating.*

"Boy, that was fun!" Caspar enthused to total silence.

It took all nine of us to pick open the knots in Ernie's skate laces.

The next day, Kristy was ready for another vigorous workout. "Okay, guys, back to the rink."

A babble of protest exploded: "Not again!"

"I'm quitting the team!"

"My uvula's busted!"

"We want Tank Command!"

"Look," said Kristy, "we didn't master it yesterday — "

"I don't see how skating makes you a better baseball player," interrupted Tuba Dave.

So out came the leg, and we got the uvula lecture again. But this time no one was buying it.

"How can I be a base stealer if I've got two broken ankles?" demanded Ryan.

"And a fractured skull!" added Luis, who had an egg-size lump on his forehead.

I played my trump card. "Caspar's a great skater. Let's see him run the bases." It was brilliant. When Caspar couldn't run any faster than the rest of us, it would prove that skating meant nothing, and my uvulas would never have to touch that ice again.

Professor Pendergast didn't remember the steal signal, even though he'd invented it. So while Caspar limbered up on first, we coached the coach. Finally, the professor was ready. He rubbed his hands over his knees and our third baseman took off like he'd been fired out of a cannon. Caspar slid into second in a cloud of dust.

"It works!" breathed Tim. "Skating works!"

"Look at the uvulas on that guy!" added Ernie.

Next we tried a game situation — Kevin on the mound, Luis behind the plate, Tuba Dave at second base. Caspar was the runner on first. They *knew* he was going to steal. They executed a perfect pitchout. But Caspar was so fast that he was practically into second before Luis could draw his arm back to throw. By the time Tuba Dave had the ball, Caspar was sliding into third.

Above our cheers and applause came the voice of Ernie McIntosh. "Can we go to the rink now?"

Kristy jogged up to Caspar. "How come you never do that during a *game*?"

Caspar shrugged uncomfortably. "I've never been on base."

"Why not?"

"I strike out a lot."

So out came Tank Command, and Caspar showed us why he'd never been a base runner. He swung too early, he swung too late. And somehow you just knew by watching him that this was as good as he was ever going to get. The sheer waste ate me up alive. His leg muscles from figure skating made him the world's greatest speedster, but he'd never get to show it.

Kristy relinquished her Tank Command seat to Tuba Dave. "You guys practice on your own. I'm going to work with Caspar, one on one."

◇

The morning of our fifth game, Kristy called up Mr. Howard to get him to take an early lunch so he wouldn't miss Caspar and the Tigers.

" 'Tsup, sir. Kristy Pendergast from New York. Assistant coach of Feather-Soft . . ."

"I hate this girl," I said aloud to no one in particular as Kristy shmoozed. *Her* team was playing a big game, and Caspar had been personally coached by *her*, and was a big part of *her* major strategy, blah, blah, blah.

Sure enough, Mr. Howard was the first guy in the bleachers that morning.

She had rearranged the entire batting order, demoting me to eighth spot. Get this — Caspar was now our leadoff man.

"Aw come on!" I whispered. "I know his dad's here, but the kid couldn't hit Ohio from downtown Cleveland! It's like starting with an automatic out!"

"Take a ride on the chill train," Kristy replied.

Our opponents were the Vic's Volvoville Wolf Pack, and they had just discovered the thirty-pound bag of sheep manure Kristy had unloaded in their dugout. Mr. Rudolph, the umpire, figured out a way to ensure that it would never happen again. He made us switch dugouts.

"Grandpa, why is Mr. Rudolph always being mean to us?" pouted the little princess.

"Just ignore it, dear," said the professor with dignity. "We'll show we're made of stronger stuff."

But there was no stuff stronger than what Kristy had dumped in the dugout. And before we could even run for a shovel, Mr. Rudolph hollered, "Play ball!"

We were down 1–0 when Caspar stepped up to

the plate to open our half of the first. Suddenly, his whole body crumpled, and he looked like a little Japanese *bonsai* tree, all twisted and gnarled. He squatted low, and doubled over at the waist, with his left shoulder six inches above the knee. The other team laughed, all except their pitcher. He was squinting in off the mound, trying to figure out where was the strike zone on this pretzel?

In the stands, Mr. Howard sat forward in confusion.

"Why's he doing that?" asked Luis.

The answer came. The first pitch was over Caspar's head; the second was in the dirt.

I knew instantly. The bat that Caspar held up by his ear, and dangled down his back, was never going to move. He was going for a base on balls.

The pitcher settled down a little and threw what I considered to be a pretty good pitch. It was still a touch too high. Ball three.

"Time out!" The Wolf Pack coach ran up to the plate, red-faced. "He's just waiting to get walked! He's not going to swing!"

Mr. Rudolph shrugged. "No crime in that."

"What about an improper batting stance?" the coach demanded.

"No such thing," replied the umpire. "Play ball."

By now the pitcher was so spooked that the fourth ball was two feet behind Caspar. He trotted down to first base. In our smelly dugout, we celebrated like this walk had been a grand slam.

On the very first pitch, the speedy Caspar stole second. The infield was powerless to stop him. One pitch later he was zooming into third.

Ernie hit a pop fly to center field, and Caspar tagged up and came home. Tie score. Now Mr. Howard understood. He was on his feet, clapping and cheering.

All that Tank Command was starting to pay off, but our defense wasn't so terrific, and Kevin's pitching, as usual, was pretty bad. I ached to pitch. But that didn't seem possible unless Mr. Lopez magically appeared to save the day.

By the end of two-and-a-half innings, the Wolf Pack was ahead, 3–2.

Looking back on it, I think the turning point in the Tigers' whole season came right then. After three weeks of a grueling crabgrass diet, Tuba Dave Jablonski stepped up to the plate, blasted the ball into the outfield, and began the long waddle to first. He was still pretty fat; he was still pretty slow; but he made it a split second before the throw.

Our bench cleared, and it had nothing to do with the sheep manure. We mobbed Tuba Dave, back-slapping and howling. Mr. Rudolph had to order us to settle down.

Predictably, Kristy took all the credit. "No biggie," she shrugged. "I said it would happen, and it happened."

Tuba Dave batted ninth, so the next man up was Caspar. He went back into that weird scrunched-up stance, and you could just tell the pitcher had been stewing about it since the first inning. He sizzled a pitch at just the right height. I thought it was a strike for sure. But Caspar's shoulder was sticking out so far that the ball grazed it. The Wolf Pack groaned. The speedster was aboard again.

Ernie came on and hit a booming drive down the first base line. Tuba Dave began waddling for third, his stubby legs pumping.

"Faster, Tuba! Faster!" screamed Kristy.

It was no use. Caspar bore down on Tuba Dave like an F-15 in a dogfight. He zoomed past, rounded third, and scored. Coming back to the bench, he looked at our agonized faces in confusion. "Aren't you going to clap?"

But it wasn't over yet. The throw from right field went wild, and Ernie decided to go for third. He slid in head first, and when he stood up and dusted himself off, there was Tuba Dave.

"What are you doing here?" Ernie demanded. "Why aren't you home?"

"I'm in the middle of a game!"

"Not that home! Home plate!"

"I'm on third!"

"*I'm* on third!"

Mr. Rudolph was totally stumped. He had to get out the rule book. And it couldn't have been easy to read with Kristy talking his ear off about how the rule book was full of beans. Caspar was out for passing a runner; Ernie was out for taking an occupied base; only Tuba Dave was safe. But he thought the inning was over, and started walking away. He was tagged out.

Kristy rallied the team. "Okay, guys, don't freak out just because we did the stupidest thing that's ever happened in a baseball game! Stay cool! We're still in this thing!"

Our secret weapon (besides the professor, who was shoveling out our dugout) was Caspar. The Wolf Pack just couldn't pitch to him. And once he was on base, there was no stopping the guy.

It kept us close. By the middle of the sixth, we were tied, 5–5.

"The game is ours to *win*!" I crowed excitedly. Then I went to the plate and promptly struck out.

Up went Tuba Dave, and he murdered the first pitch. It sailed away — right into the center fielder's glove.

Now there were two out, and we pinned all our hopes on Caspar Howard. Would the master come through yet again, maintain his sparkling .000 average, and get yet another walk?

Only — something happened that hadn't happened all game. The pitcher floated a slow, straight ball just above Caspar's knees.

"Strike one!" bawled Mr. Rudolph.

"Fluke!" screeched Kristy.

The fluke happened again, same pitch, same place.

"Strike two!"

Kristy sat down in disgust. "What a rip-off! We couldn't even get a whole game out of our miracle!"

The Wolf Pack pitcher lofted the identical throw and you could tell he had solved the Caspar mystery.

From the bleachers came Mr. Howard's cry. *"Swing!!"*

Caspar swung, a halfhearted little chop. But it connected. It was almost like a bunt, a weak dribbler out toward the mound. The pitcher and catcher both went for it, meeting with a resounding crunch. The pitcher's throw to first was high. And by the time the Wolf Pack got things under control, there stood Caspar in his usual spot, on third base.

Kristy sent Ernie up to the plate with a message — hit or die. All eyes focussed on the plate. You could have heard a pin drop — that and the sound of Professor Pendergast's shovel scraping against the cement steps. Poor old guy. He was a top scientist, a renowned genius, working like a stable hand, without a word of complaint. He tossed his shovel aside and stepped out to the field where he stood, brushing off his pants.

It hit me in one instant of exquisite horror — *that was the steal sign*!

Caspar the human bullet fired himself down the third base line.

"No-o-o-o-o!" cried Kristy.

It unfolded like a nightmare. The pitcher threw. Ernie swung and missed. There stood the Wolf Pack catcher, astride the plate, ball in hand, waiting to make the tag.

"I can't look!" howled Kevin.

Ten feet from home, our third baseman launched himself into the air in a spectacular leap. It was way too early for a slide, but figure skaters can do almost anything in midair. For a second he was up there, and the catcher was reaching out for the tag. But suddenly, Caspar dropped, diving headfirst between the defender's legs, in a shower of dirt. When the dust cleared, there lay the runner, his hand on home plate.

Final score, 6–5, Tigers.

CHAPTER ⟨7⟩

Center Field —
Tim Laredo

When we told Professor Pendergast we'd won, he didn't believe us! So we showed him the scoreboard, but it said 6–5 for the home team, and we were in the visitors' dugout. For a minute there I questioned it myself. We were so great at losing — maybe I'd counted wrong.

But then Kristy remembered the big dugout switch, and we knew it was true. Victory. Very sweet.

The professor was so excited you'd have thought he'd seen another antilepton. He got an eighty-dollar speeding ticket taking us out to lunch.

I walked on air all day. I ate, drank, and breathed baseball. I talked nonstop about our first win. And when my folks couldn't stand me anymore, I watched baseball on TV. Then I rented *The Babe*

Ruth Story and watched that. When that ended, there was no more baseball in the house except my dad's video of Little League from last year. So I popped it into the VCR, and feasted on me, Tim, and Tuba Dave on the Gunhold Auto Body Blue Jays. The Jays had won about half their games, but not one single "W" had meant as much as today.

" 'Tsup?"

I was almost glad to see her — someone from the Tigers, a connection to our triumph.

She joined me in front of the TV. "Hey, that's you. You looked pretty geeky as a little kid. Check out those ears!"

"Shut up," I said in a friendly fashion. I was still mellow.

"Thought you were a pitcher," she commented.

I was playing third base on the video. "I started practicing over the winter. I figured I'd pitch this summer."

She nodded sympathetically. "I know what you mean. I always wanted to be a movie star. Reality sandwich." She pointed at the screen. "Hey, there's Tuba Dave! He was always fat."

I sighed. Suddenly I'd had enough baseball for one day.

But Kristy was really into the video. "Wow, look at that kid! What a fielder! Boffo arm! Wish the Tigers had him."

"We do," I replied. "It's Tim."

"In his dreams!" she sneered. "No way that's Tim."

I fast-forwarded to where we were at bat. Sure enough, good old number nine, Tim Laredo, belted a stand-up double.

Kristy was furious. "The nerve of that guy! Why can't he play like that for *us*?"

That was a good question. Tim was okay as a Tiger, but I guess I'd forgotten that he'd been one of the Jays' best players. Very good question.

"He isn't injured." I mused. "He isn't out of shape — he played sports all winter."

Kristy ejected the tape and headed up the stairs. "Come on, Johnson. We've got work to do."

I folded my arms. "I refuse to go over there and bug Tim."

"This is a social call," she insisted. "We'll say 'tsup, max and relax, talk about the game, the weather, how he went from all-star to insect in one short year — "

I had to go with her, just to protect Tim.

"Def crib, bro'," approved Kristy, looking with an appraiser's eye around the room Tim shared with his brother, Terence the Terrorist.

Tim looked bewildered. "Crib?"

"You know — place, pad, digs, spread. Room," she added. She pointed to a strip of masking tape that stretched from wall to wall, more or less down the middle of the floor. "Yo, man, what's with the stripe?"

Tim looked sheepish. "That's the dividing line. Terence likes to keep our parts of the room separate."

"I notice he took the bigger half," I couldn't resist pointing out.

Uncomfortably, Tim changed the subject. "I'm still shaking from the game! What an ending!"

"Speaking of baseball," Kristy eased into her topic with the subtlety of a rampaging hippo. "How come you used to be so great and now you stink?"

"Oh, come on!" I blurted.

"Well, he's bound to know," she reasoned. "He's the one doing the stinking." She waved the video in Tim's face. "You were awesome last year! I was impressed, and I'm from New York! This year you're not terrible, but you're — you know — no better than Johnson here. 'Tsupwitchoo?"

I took it personally. "Hey!"

Tim looked unhappy. "You're right. I'm trying as hard as last year, but it's just not working out. Maybe the League got better and I stayed the same."

Kristy frowned. "What's different from last year?"

In the kitchen, the refrigerator door slammed. *"Hey, butt-brain! Who ate the rest of the chicken?"*

Tim went white to the ears. "It's Terence the Terrorist! Quick! Hide!"

116

"I'm not afraid of him," said Kristy.

Tim jammed both of us under his bed, which was a good thing because I *was!* "He hits the roof when I bring people here!"

"We're on your half," Kristy pointed out.

But before he could answer, the door flew open and in roared Tim's sixteen-year-old brother, in a rage as usual.

"Did you eat my chicken?"

"Who said if was *your* chicken?" Tim argued feebly.

"Because everything is mine! And nothing is yours!"

"Here," offered Tim. "I've got a chocolate bar."

Terence snatched it out of his hand. "If I get a zit, you're dead!"

"Not a reasonable guy," whispered Kristy under the bed.

"Shhh," I cautioned. The mattress was sagging in my face.

"All right, who moved my paperweight?" Terence demanded.

"I didn't touch it," said Tim. "It's on the desk where it always is."

"It's supposed to be in the *middle*! It's way over to the *side*! How many times do I have to tell you? Quit messing with my stuff!"

There was a loud ripping sound, and then Tim exclaimed, "Aw, come on Terrence, not again!"

The Terrorist stormed off, slamming the door behind him.

We scrambled out of our hiding place.

"Are you okay?" I asked. "What did he do to you?"

"He deducted another six inches from my side of the room," said Tim mournfully.

We looked at the tape. It was now just a little closer to Tim's bed.

"Claustrophobia city, man," Kristy commented. "And as for baseball — it's pretty obvious. Your problem is your brother."

"That's stupid!" Tim exploded. "He's never even seen me play!"

"Psychology, bro'," Kristy explained. "He's always in your face, and you can't get away from him because you live together. So on the field you think you're giving a hundred percent, but you're really not because the Terrorist has got you spooked."

"That doesn't explain last season," I put in. "Terence was his brother then, too, and Tim played great."

"Johnson, you're not as stupid as you look," Kristy praised me. "Maybe the answer is not what's different about Tim, but what's different about Terence."

"Well," said our center fielder thoughtfully. "He has been a lot meaner since his girlfriend dumped him."

Kristy grinned broadly. "Then that's the focus of our attack."

"Attack?!" I squeaked. "Are you crazy? Don't you remember what he did to me after I hit him with the baseball?"

"He's soft," she snorted. "There he was with a chain saw, and all he did was punch you. He's history."

The *Spooner Gazette* was our daily paper — not bad for a smaller town. Even though most people read the Dallas papers for real news, all of Spooner subscribed to *The Gazette* to find out who was born and who died. Next to the obits, the favorite column in town was "Grandma Lacey," who was our version of Ann Landers.

At practice on Tuesday, Casper was showing us how to slide into a base under the tag, when Kristy ran up, waving *The Gazette,* hooting and snickering. She called Tim and me over to the dugout, and showed us today's "Grandma Lacey."

Dear Grandma Lacey,
    I am a sixteen-year-old girl from a farm north of Spooner. The last time I was in town, I got a wax job at Lone Star Car Wash, and I was waited on by

the most gorgeous guy. He was very tall with blond hair and a red muscle-shirt. I can't stop thinking about him. What should I do? He doesn't even know I'm alive!

Signed: Smitten in Spooner

Dear S in S,

Your young man is Terence Laredo, who'll be a senior at Spooner High this fall.

Terence, if you're out there, there's someone who wants to meet you, tee-hee!

Lacey

Tim looked puzzled. "Who'd write a letter like that about Terence?"

"I wrote it, stupid!" exclaimed Kristy. "It's part of our plan!"

"Our plan is to give him even more of a swelled head than he already has?" I said in disbelief.

She turned to face the side of the dugout. "Hello, wall," she said to the cement. "Pay attention, dudes. The Terrorist got evil when his chick gave him the heave-ho. So we've got to convince the guy that women dig him again."

"But Terence doesn't read the paper," said Tim.

"I don't think he's ever even finished a book unless somebody was forcing him."

"Don't worry," laughed Kristy. "A hick town like this is like living in a fishbowl. Someone'll tell him." She ran off and disappeared into the phone booth.

Tim looked nervous. "I hope she isn't going to try to mess with Terence like she does with us!"

"It won't work," I concluded. "Terence isn't in The Picture."

All afternoon Kristy hung around my house like a bad smell. And every time I tried to kick her out, she'd start up a conversation with my mother and act like my closest friend. I couldn't get rid of her.

". . . so stay tuned to Spooner's own KSPN, country ninety-one," came the voice over the radio. "This next song goes out to Terence, over at Lone Star Car Wash, from your secret admirer. Here's 'I've Got My Eye on You'."

I groaned. "*Now* are you going to go home?"

"We're just getting started," she retorted. "What other towns have radio stations around here?"

I shrugged. "Athens, Tyler. Some people can even get Dallas."

"We'll call them all, just to be on the safe side."

And she did. "To Terence from Kiki in the red Corvette," "To the Hunk of the Car Wash," "To

121

T. L. from the French exchange student," and so on.

Then she called up our afternoon phone-in show, *Spooner Talks*. In a perfect East Texas accent with not a "yo" or " 'tsup" in sight, she pledged undying love for the hot wax guy at Lone Star Car Wash.

The host asked, "Not the same boy who was written up in today's 'Grandma Lacey'?"

Instantly, Kristy hung up. "We have liftoff."

Kristy was right. The news got through to Terence. According to Tim, The Terrorist was constantly up at his dresser, staring at himself in the mirror.

"Was he any nicer than usual?" asked Kristy.

"Nicer?" repeated Tim. "He was horrible. First he said that I'd never be popular like him. Then he blamed me for fogging up his mirror, and he slammed a dictionary shut on my nose and deducted a whole foot from my half of the room! I can hardly stand beside my bed!"

"Well, I guess that's that," I said hopefully. Of all Kristy's weird plans, this one seemed the most bizarre.

"This is going to work," she told us. "Trust me."

It probably wasn't a coincidence that there was a little something extra on the Lone Star Car Wash flyers that went out to every house in town:

LONE STAR CAR WASH
FEATURING
TERENCE ON WAX.

"How did you pull if off?" I asked as we gathered up the equipment after practice.

"Simple," she replied. "Ry sweeps up at the print shop at night. I got him to do it. He knows he got off easy on the ranch thing. Hang out."

She expected me to stand there while she carved Terence's initials into a telephone pole.

"Why won't you just admit this is stupid?" I challenged. "It's not going to work."

"Wanna bet?"

"Strangest thing I ever saw," said Mr. Hofstetler, owner of Lone Star Car Wash. He indicated a dozen freshly washed vehicles waiting in the wax line. "All the teenage girls in this town are bringing their fathers' cars in. Why today?"

Kristy shrugged. "It's drive-in season. Everybody wants to look hype."

Mr. Hofstetler was unconvinced. "They could have been out of here an hour ago. I've got waxers sitting around doing nothing. The customers are all asking for the Laredo boy."

I shuffled uncomfortably. "Maybe he's a good worker."

The owner shook his head. "A wax job is a wax job."

Kristy glanced over at Terence, who was hardly working at all. His polishing cloth barely moved as he flirted with the pretty blonde driver of a Dodge pickup. "He's box office," she explained.

"Box office!?" Mr. Hofstetler repeated. "He's a waxer, not a movie star!"

"We New Yorkers know these things," Kristy assured him. "See?" she added as the pickup driver slipped Terence her phone number and drove off.

At that moment, a rusty old station wagon rattled up. "We have to have Terence," insisted the driver as three of her friends convulsed with giggles. "We'll wait."

Kristy shrugged. "It's not what he does; it's how he does it. He has *aura*, man!"

A pyramid of crumpled up notes and phone numbers rose from Terence's desk. The scent of aftershave was in the air. We could hear Mrs. Laredo on the telephone in the kitchen. "Sorry, Wendy, Terence is out for the evening. . . ."

I wondered if he was with the pickup truck, the four-by-four, or the Buick convertible.

Kristy was stretched out on Terence's bed, reading his calendar, and chortling. " 'Lunch with Carol,'

'Coffee break with Ashley,' 'Dinner with Kiki,' 'Movies with Wanda.' " She turned to Tim. "I guess *your* life must be getting a lot easier."

"No way!" Tim groaned. "He's worse than ever!"

Kristy frowned. "Where does he get the time?"

"He *makes* the time," said Tim bitterly. "He comes back from those dates so bigheaded that I'm nothing but dirt under his feet!"

I checked the dividing line. The masking tape now came out from the wall eighteen inches from Tim's bed. From there, it cut sharply in, forming a tiny box around the bed and desk. Tim had to cross his brother's territory just to get to the closet.

At practice, he was having even more problems than before. And it didn't help that Terence had an upcoming date with Ernie's older sister.

"Can I trust your brother?" Ernie bugged Tim during Tank Command. "What are his intentions?"

"Will you leave me alone?" Tim exploded. He got the next tennis ball right in his face.

"But he's taking out my sister!" Ernie explained.

Kristy threw her arms wide. "He's taking out *everybody's* sister!"

Lone Star Car Wash was the hottest ticket in Spooner. It was an hour wait for a wax job. The streets looked like Beverly Hills, each car gleaming brighter than the next. I saw a Chevy that must have been older than my dad — it was roaring along at five miles per hour, dragging a broken muffler. And it was shinier than a brand-new Rolls-Royce.

It was all Terence. Across town at Wash 'n Wax, business was practically zero.

"This is your fault!" I accused Kristy. "Mr. Hofstetler's getting rich, Wash 'n Wax is going out of business, and Tim can hardly catch a fly ball!"

Kristy nodded. "I guess it's time to put our plan into the final phase."

"Plan?" I repeated. "Surely you're not telling me you *planned* all this?"

She shrugged airily. "We New Yorkers are always ready to wing it."

Dear Grandma Lacey,

 I've been a big fan of Terence Laredo, but I just found out that he's mean to his little brother. I think that, for a guy with as much going for him as Terence has, picking on a little kid is just plain sad, and I refuse to pay good money to get my car waxed by a slimeball.

  Signed: No More Wax Jobs

Dear NMWJ,
  If what you say is true, it certainly
seems like our Terence has some grow-
ing up to do!
                    Lacey

Kristy did the whole thing in reverse. She called up all those radio stations again. I figured no one gets on the air to complain about a bully. Wrong. Terence was so famous that even the deejays knew about him. In a couple of hours, Kristy had a first-class scandal brewing.

There was resistance, especially from girls who still had dates coming up. So Kristy, ever the photographer, took a picture of the Laredo boys' room. She carefully diagrammed whose side was whose, showing how Tim was being squeezed out. This she brought to Grandma Lacey herself, and it was published in the next day's *Gazette*, under the headline: "TERENCE, YOU LET US DOWN."

There was a miniriot at the car wash. Terence was pelted with sponges, and called every name in the book.

"Take the rest of the day off, son," advised Mr. Hofstetler kindly.

So Terence went home to find out that things weren't any better there. The phone was ringing off the hook — date breakers and angry ex-fans who wanted to give Terence a piece of their minds. A few of them were even coming to the door, demanding to speak to their former hero. A sign mysteriously appeared on the lawn:

TERENCE LAREDO UNFAIR TO TIM

Mrs. Laredo tried calling the police to complain about the harassment. She got a lecture about the way she and her husband had let Terence run roughshod over his younger brother — which made pretty good sense to me, actually.

Terence was on the edge. "This can't be legal! We can sue Grandma Lacey!"

"I already spoke to my lawyer," said Mr. Laredo bitterly. "You know what he gave me? A message from his daughter. You and she are *off* for dinner Saturday night, Lover Boy!"

Kristy and I were hiding under Tim's bed.

"You hear that?" I hissed. "This is *nuts*! If Terence ever finds out who's behind it, Tim's dead!"

Kristy shrugged. "So long as the baseball season's over, that's Tim's problem."

Terence came stomping in, slamming the door, and cracking the frame. "Has the whole world gone crazy?" he howled. "They're screaming for my head out there! They want me to get the electric chair over a dumb piece of masking tape!"

Even Tim felt bad for his brother. "I'm sorry, Terence."

"Thanks, kid," quavered the Terrorist. "You're the only friend I've got left. And the worst part is — I don't know how any of this happened to me!"

Kristy scrambled out from under the bed. "I did it."

The Terrorist's eyes bulged. "You?"

I emerged just in time to see Kristy unfold a paper and present it to Terence. It was a photocopy of the original Grandma Lacey letter.

Tim was ashen. I guess he was afraid his brother would go berserk and slaughter us all. I figured Tim's half of the room would be reduced to three square inches in a corner of the closet.

But Terence was paralyzed with horror, looking from the copy to Kristy, and back to the copy again. "But — but how?" he managed finally.

She shrugged modestly. "People talk, rumors spread. I built you up, I took you down. No biggie."

"Why?"

"Baseball," said Kristy.

"Baseball!?" Terence was totally bewildered.

Kristy put a protective arm around Tim. "My center fielder was stinking the joint out because a certain big brother was in his face and on his case. So I solved the problem."

"By doing *this*?"

Kristy was impatient. "If we'd've come to you like *oh-please-big-brother*, you'd've laughed in our faces, right?"

Terence was beyond speech.

"Cheer up, bro'," Kristy grinned. "This is your lucky day. I'm gonna get you off the hook. But remember — I can do it all again in two seconds. One wrong move and you're dissed like dirt!"

Terence stared at her. "Dissed?"

"You know, up the creek, nailed, rocked, stabbed and slabbed, zonked, keel-hauled." He still looked confused. She said, "You'll figure it out," and left, dragging me with her.

Dear Grandma Lacey,

My name is Tim Laredo, and I'm the younger brother of Terence Laredo, who you write about so much. I just want to say that Terence is a great guy and not mean at all. As for the masking tape, our house is built over an underground river, and we like to mark the line of the riverbed. Thanks to you and to my friend Kristy (from New York) for helping to work all this out.

Signed: Tim Laredo

Dear Tim,
   Thanks for setting the record straight.
Terence, we never doubted you for a
second!
                           Lacey

I looked up from the paper. "Do we have under-ground rivers in Texas?"

"Who cares?" She pointed to the outfield, where Tim was catching fly balls and firing them to second without a hop. "We've got our star center fielder."

In a way, she was right. But did the end justify the means? I couldn't get Terence's words out of my mind. According to Tim, right after we left, the fearsome Terrorist turned to him and said, "Some people curse you out, give you dirty looks, maybe even pick a fight. Her? She ruins your life!"

CHAPTER 8

Shortstop — Bobby Ray Devereaux

Tim came on like a house on fire. In our next game he was awesome — batting 3 for 4, and throwing two runners out on monster heaves from center field. With Caspar burning up the base paths, and Tuba Dave making it to first more and more often, we killed the Mr. Halibut Fish and Chips Minutemen 8–2.

"They're as bad as you guys *used* to be!" Kristy said, just in case we were considering being proud of ourselves.

Two runs was the fewest we'd allowed all season. Kevin wasn't getting any better. But Bobby Ray Devereaux, our shortstop, had the game of his life. You'd hear the crack of the bat — and out of nowhere, there was Bobby Ray! He'd nab it in the air, or turn it into a double play, or get the ball to Luis for a tag at the plate. He was a one-man infield!

And a total loss at bat. He struck out twice, grounded out, and to cap it off, bunted foul on the third strike. He was hopeless.

" 'Tsupwitchoor bat, bro'?" challenged Kristy after the game. "Does it have bad breath, so all the baseballs won't go near it?"

Bobby Ray didn't get it. "I beg your pardon?"

"Your fielding is *fly,* but your batting is toiletsville!"

He shuffled uncomfortably. "I'm not much of a hitter."

"Sure you are!" I put in. "Just last game you went three for three!"

Our shortstop looked mystified. "I did?"

Ernie couldn't believe it. "Don't you remember? That's the day you made five errors."

"Oh, right," Bobby Ray agreed quickly. And he ran off.

"All right, Johnson. What's the tip on him?"

I shrugged. "You know what we know. He goes to school in Eaton, so we don't see him much."

"His dad runs the gas station on Route 17," put in Kevin. "He helps out sometimes."

Kristy was wary. "He isn't another Fortune 500 kind of helper?" She indicated Ryan.

"It's a small station," said Kevin. "He washes windshields and stuff."

"Let's get in his face," Kristy decided.

She wanted us to *phone* Bobby Ray — day and night — to bug him about his hitting, and lecture on team loyalty.

"Aw, come on!" I cried, but everybody else thought it was a great idea!

"I think we should trust her," said Caspar when she was gone. "I used to hate baseball, but, thanks to her, I'm really having fun."

I couldn't believe my ears. "What about all that stuff she pulled? What about *horta*?"

"I used to be batting zero," said Tuba Dave. "Now I'm already over .200."

"She's a blackmailing sleazeball!" I grimaced. "What about The Picture?"

"She only does that stuff because she likes us, and she loves the professor, and she wants the Tigers to have a good season," Ernie explained.

"Oh, I get it," I said sarcastically. "All that rottenness is really niceness in disguise."

"Yesterday she caught me eating a doughnut at the mall," put in Tuba Dave, "and she really helped me get back on the diet."

That I couldn't believe. "How?"

"She dumped a bottle of Hershey's syrup over my head, and then she made me eat four bowls of *horta* before she agreed not to make eight hundred copies of The Picture."

I threw my arms up in dismay. "You guys are

losing touch with reality! You need Mr. Lopez to straighten all this out!"

"Who's Mr. Lopez?" queried Ernie.

"The League president!" I exploded. "The guy I complained to!"

Tuba Dave stared at me in horror. "You mean you didn't write back and cancel the complaint?"

"Of course not! The complaint counts now more than ever!"

"Well," said Tim hopefully, "maybe the letter got lost in the mail so Kristy can stay."

And no matter how hard I tried, I just couldn't convince those guys that Kristy wasn't their best friend. My only hope was that Mr. Lopez *would* come. Then, once we had our team back, they'd realize how much better it was without Kristy.

Little League rules state that a pitcher has to have three days' rest between starts. Our next game was only two days later, so Kevin wasn't eligible.

I worked on the professor night and day. I hung around his house; I even made friendly small talk with Kristy. And it paid off. The night before the game, our coach agreed that I was the logical choice. Best of all, he said it right in front of his little princess. It was a glorious moment.

But come game time, when the roster was handed to Mr. Rudolph, *Tim* was the pitcher.

I hit the ceiling. "*You* did this!" I roared at Kristy. "After the coach promised I'd get the start!"

She didn't even bother fighting with me. "Looks like rain," she commented, glancing up.

It was the worst insult of all.

We were at bat first. Caspar got his usual walk, but there was no chance to steal second. Bobby Ray smashed the first pitch for a two-run homer.

Kristy took all the credit. "See? You lean on the dude and he comes through for you."

Then we took our 2–0 lead to the field. We were better off with Kevin on the mound. Tim had a good arm, sure. But all he could throw were straight fastballs. The Wiley's Cafeteria and Ammo Supply Cardinals were hitting him all over the place. In no time the bases were loaded, with only one out.

"Do I pitch like that?" called Kevin from center field.

"Nah," I replied. "You *walk* the bases full!"

We got lucky. The batter hit a weak grounder to shortstop — the perfect double play ball, to our best infielder.

Bobby Ray reached down to scoop it up, and the dribbler rolled under his glove, between his legs, and out toward left field. But our shortstop must have thought he had it — he actually reached into his glove, pulled out nothing, and tried to throw it home. By this time, I was barreling *in* after the ball, and Bobby Ray was running *out* for it. We met with a *crunch!* and I saw stars. By the time they cleared away, we were behind 4–2, and Kristy was looking murderously down at me.

"Yo, Johnson! Give the kid some space. He's only the best shortstop in the league!"

But if Bobby Ray was such a great shortstop, why was he playing like a confused baboon? I stopped counting his errors when he hit double digits. He bobbled grounders. He missed line drives. He booted the ball all over the infield. When he did make a catch, he threw to the wrong base, or into the stands. He lobbed one into our dugout that had the professor diving for his life.

The really weird part was his hitting was amazing! He had two homers, a double, and a single. So both teams were running up huge scores! *Us* because Bobby Ray was such a monster at the plate. And *them* because of Tim's pitching, and our gigantic hole at shortstop. The lead flip-flopped all game, 5–4 us, 8–6 them, 10–9 us, 13–11 them, and so on. Who made the difference? The weather. Because the thunderstorm hit after five innings with the Tigers ahead 15–14. The Cardinals were so heartbroken they left! We, the victors, had to lay down the waterproof ground sheet to cover the pitcher's mound. We got drenched.

"I can't believe I was the winning pitcher!" Tim exclaimed, rain beating off the visor of his cap. "I allowed fourteen runs!"

At least he got to pitch.

We got out of there just before the scoreboard got struck by lightning.

◇

The next day, I woke up determined to earn the job of pitcher for the Toilet Paper Tigers. The problem was that *I* knew I was better than Kevin and Tuba Dave and Tim, but nobody else did. I finally figured out a way to show them. I'd pretend to be helping Luis with his catching. Then I'd throw him my best stuff — my fastball, my change-up, and maybe even the curve I'd been working on in the spring. Luis would tell the guys how good I was, and the professor would have to put me in, no matter what Kristy said.

Right after breakfast, I rapped smartly on Luis's door. His mom answered.

"Hi, Mrs. Bono. Is Luis around?"

"You just missed him, Corey," she told me. "He's on his way to Kristy's house."

Kristy's house? What would Luis be doing there? I frowned. She was up to something again.

As I headed over to the professor's place, I wondered if this had anything to do with The Picture. I quickened my pace to a jog.

The professor let me in. "Kristy will be right with you, Corey. She's on the phone with her mother."

He showed me into the living room. There, polishing off a tall glass of milk, sat Luis.

"What's going on?" I whispered.

Luis looked perplexed. "Nothing. Why?"

"What'd she say to you?"

Luis raised an eyebrow.

"To get you to come here!" I persisted.

Luis shrugged. "I just figured since there's no game or practice, she might want to go swimming, or to the mall, or something."

The doorbell rang and, a moment later, our coach was ushering Ernie and Tuba Dave into the living room.

I stared at my three teammates. "You mean, you guys are all here — *on purpose*?"

Tuba Dave nodded. "Where's Kristy?"

At that moment, Kristy's voice swelled from the kitchen. "Just because you and Dad came home early doesn't mean I have to! I'm having a great time! I've got tons of friends down here!"

I threw my hands up in exasperation. "Can't you guys tell a snow job when you hear one? She's not talking to her parents! It's all an act for *us*! I'll bet there's no one on the other end. See?" I picked up an extension phone and listened for the dial tone.

Instead, Kristy's voice barked, "Put it down, or forfeit your arm!"

"See?" said Ernie. "She really *is* on the phone. And she likes it here."

"Sure," I said coldly. "That's why she calls us hicks and hayseeds."

" 'Tsup, dudes?" Kristy rolled in from the kitchen.

" 'Tsup?" chorused Ernie, Tuba Dave, and Luis. I rolled my eyes.

"Got any plans for your day off?" asked Tuba Dave.

"What day off?" scoffed Kristy. "We've got *mucho* biz today."

"Biz?" I repeated.

"Business," she explained. "Check it out. How could a guy be a Golden Glove hype shortstop and a useless hitter on Tuesday, and by Thursday, he's forgotten how to field, but he hits like Joe DiMaggio?"

"You mean Bobby Ray?" asked Ernie.

"Word," she nodded. "I've finally figured out his problem. He's crazy."

I was angry. "Are you sure you're not reading the file marked KRISTY PENDERGAST?"

"That's cold, man," she pretended to be hurt. "Here I am trying to help the team and you're *dissing* me."

"Look who's talking!" I exploded. "You just called the kid crazy! He never did anything to you!"

"I don't mean crazy like an insult!" she exclaimed. "I mean *really* crazy. Haven't you ever heard of a split personality? Like one minute you're an accountant, the next you're an ax murderer?"

"Hey, yeah!" exclaimed Tuba Dave. "I once heard of this lady in Arkansas — sometimes she was a nun, sometimes she thought she was a gorilla in the Congo! They caught her up on her roof trying to bean people with coconuts!"

"That's Bobby Ray," confirmed Kristy.

"We don't even know if he likes coconuts," Ernie protested.

"Look, if you can be a nun *and* a gorilla, you can also be a great shortstop *and* a great hitter. Split personality."

"Why just two personalities?" I said sarcastically. "Maybe he's a hitter and a shortstop *and* a gorilla! And in his spare time, he's Elvis!"

But my teammates were already congratulating Kristy on her brilliant diagnosis.

"Boy, I sure never would've thought of that," said Luis.

"Poor Bobby Ray," added Ernie.

I had to admit that she sort of had a point. I thought back to when Bobby Ray couldn't even remember his performance from last game. And split personality *was* a real thing. "Let's say you're right. What do we do?"

"It's a delicate situation," Kristy lectured like she'd just graduated from psychology school. From a bookcase she pulled a well-thumbed paperback entitled *Disorders of the Mind.* "The hitter personality doesn't know about the shortstop part, and vice versa. Our job is to kind of *introduce* the two parts."

"How do we do that?" asked Ernie, wide-eyed.

"It's not in the book," Kristy admitted. "But I figure if we talk about different games we've played, he'll have to jump back and forth from personality to personality so fast that it'll all meld into one."

"And once he's cured," added Tuba Dave, "we'll have a hitter and a shortstop at the same time."

"He'll be *the real deal,*" she promised.

Bobby Ray lived in a town called Steep Rock Lake, halfway between Spooner and Eaton. Actually, Steep Rock Lake was a gas station, but it was outside the city limits, so it got to be its own town. Mr. Devereaux ran the station, and he and Bobby Ray were the only people who lived there.

Luis had an extra bike for Kristy, so the five of us rode out after lunch.

There wasn't much traffic on Route 17 since they built the Interstate, so the Devereaux gas station was deserted when we got there. We sat on our bikes for a few minutes, waiting to be noticed.

"He must be in the grease pit," Kristy decided, indicating the auto shop beside the gas pump. "Wait here."

She disappeared, and we rode up to the pumps.

All four of us rolled over the black hose, but only Tuba Dave was heavy enough to ring the bell.

"Aw, c'mon!" he groaned. "Five weeks of crabgrass, and I'm still heavy as a car!"

The bell was the signal that there were customers. On cue, Bobby Ray emerged from the house.

I waved to our shortstop, shouting "I found him!" into the auto shop.

At first I thought it was an echo. Kristy hollered "I found him!" right along with me.

"*You* found him? He's right here!"

That was when Kristy stepped out into the sunlight — *with Bobby Ray*! I looked back to the house. There was Bobby Ray. There were two of him!

Ernie gasped in horror. "Clones!"

Kristy had it right away. "Twins, dummy!" She stepped back. "Right? One's the hitter, one's the shortstop."

The two Bobby Rays exchanged agonized glances. "I'm Billy Ray," the one by me said finally. "He's Bobby Joe. We kind of averaged our names."

Kristy nodded wisely. "And you switched games, pretending to be one dude."

"So it looked like a guy who never played the same way twice," added Luis.

That also explained why "Bobby Ray" could never remember the last game.

"We're sorry," said Bobby Joe, studying the tarmac.

"But why?" asked Kristy. "Why couldn't you both play?"

Billy Ray studied his shoelaces. "There's not much business on Route 17 anymore. Our dad just couldn't pay for both of us."

"We were wrong," said Billy Ray. "The Tigers could've gotten in big trouble because of us. We just both wanted to play so bad, and since we look alike — " He turned to his brother. "You can finish the season. At least you can hit."

Bobby Joe shrugged. "Let's let Kristy decide. She's the coach."

I let that one pass. I felt so bad for the twins — I knew how much playing baseball meant to me. I'd always taken the money part for granted.

The other guys felt the same way. "You haven't been caught all summer," shrugged Luis. "Why not just keep on switching games?"

"I've got a better idea," said Kristy. "We'll use you both *every* game. You can change halfway through."

"It's too bad we can't switch them every half inning," I put in, mostly just to see what she'd say. "That way we'd always have Billy Ray at short, and Bobby Joe at bat."

"No way," said Kristy sternly. "The great Tigers — with a *New Yorker* behind them — don't need to break any rules to kick everybody's butt down here in the boondocks."

I couldn't believe my ears! "Look who's Miss Fair Play all of a sudden! Gee, you have a short memory! What about trying to hypnotize the ump? Or tripping a runner? Or putting sheep manure in the visitors' dugout?"

"Yo, bro', if you can show me where there's a Little League rule against sheep manure, I'll tear up The Picture and burn the negative." She was triumphant. "So we'll start Billy Ray, and play Bobby Joe as a tenth man — just so long as we don't put in the twin who's been taken out."

Billy Ray had a sensible comment. "It's still illegal. We only paid for one kid."

"And only one kid is playing," she replied with an expansive shrug. "One at a time, that is." She looked pleased. "How about that? We finally have a substitute."

◇

She had no problem explaining it to the professor. She just said, "Look, Grandpa, Bobby Ray has a twin!" and our coach welcomed the newcomer and went back to not understanding the game.

"Hey!" I hissed. "I thought you were going to tell him the plan!"

"That info comes on a 'need-to-know' basis," replied Agent Kristy of the CIA. "How could he need to know something that's only going to get him all confused?"

The "hype tip" (her words, not mine) was to start Billy Ray, so his brilliant defense would keep us from falling too far behind.

". . . meanwhile, Bobby Joe's chilling in the washroom hut," Kristy explained. "Halfway through the game, when you gotta go, you gotta go! Billy Ray boogies to the can. They switch jerseys, and we've got Bobby Joe's bat to blow the other team away."

We went on a tear, smashing the competition. Even the professor was starting to get the hang of it. He still didn't know anything about baseball, but he sensed the excitement of the players. And a man of science sure couldn't miss the numbers we were putting on the scoreboard!

We even got crowds. Not huge crowds, but the word was spreading among our families that the Feather-Soft Tigers were actually *winning* a few games. We acquired fans from Ryan's ex-jobs, too, mostly the paper routes. But Mr. Cacciatore became a regular booster. He even brought Big Al to a game. (Mr. Featherstone had to buy the league a new ball after Big Al *ate* a foul tip — no kidding!)

It was amazing! Not only *didn't* we stink — we were *great*! The two Devereaux twins made up the best one player in the league. Caspar was easily the fastest. Tim was very good, and the new, improved, crabgrass-eating Tuba Dave was a powerhouse! With the rest of us working hard and improving, the Tigers won four in a row, extending our streak to seven.

It was neat to be the hottest team around. It didn't even bother me so much that I was stuck out in left field. Back in June, I'd have been amazed if someone had told me we'd win a single game. Now we were almost stars. The other teams knew us, looked up to us, dreamed of beating us.

I'm not trying to say "and they all lived happily ever after." It wasn't perfect. I still thought a lot about pitching. But when Kevin got a sore arm in the fifth inning, Ernie came in, not me. Another time it was a Devereaux — I forget which one. Even Caspar faced one batter. I stayed in left field.

Of course, the biggest frustration of all was that we were too far behind to make the playoffs. Only the four best records in the whole county advanced to postseason. Last year, even the third and fourth spots had gone to teams with only three losses all summer.

But it was *fun*. Our last game was like a big celebration. We scored twelve runs in a huge victory, and every guy crossed the plate at least once. Our families gave us a standing ovation.

Even Mr. Rudolph was impressed. He shook hands solemnly with the professor. "Pendergast, you turned these boys into a real team. I'm nominating you for Coach of the Year."

The professor beamed. "I enjoyed every single touchdown."

We laughed. Everything was funny. Everything was great.

Then there was a party at the professor's house. We gave "three cheers" for the professor, and then for Mr. Featherstone, our sponsor. And everyone was bragging about how, if we'd made the playoffs, we'd have killed the competition. It's easy to make promises you don't have to keep.

" 'Tsup?" Kristy approached, working on a chocolate ice cream rootbeer float. "Hey, check out Tuba Dave. He's chowing down."

I laughed a little. "That's because he's off *horta* for the first time in months." I glanced at her. She was smiling, and joking, and friendly — she didn't seem to know that she and I had been fighting nonstop since Day One. Suddenly, I blurted, "Kristy, why do you hate me so much?"

"I don't hate anybody."

"Come on!" I scoffed. "You knew I wanted to pitch, and you made sure I never got near the mound! On purpose! Even when Kevin couldn't start, you went out of your way not to put me in! You were practically dragging relief pitchers in off the street! Why? What did I ever do to you?"

Wordlessly, she reached into her back pocket, pulled out a tattered piece of paper, and handed it to me. I unfolded it and gawked. It was a photocopy of my letter to Mr. Lopez.

"The league forwarded it to P.P." She shrugged. "I didn't want to bother him with details." She looked at me earnestly. "That was a lousy thing to do, Johnson. It really hurt."

"How — how do you know *I* wrote it?"

She laughed in my face. "Get real! 'Not letting people pitch!' Who else could it be?"

I felt pretty stupid. It had seemed so clever at the time!

"What was the crime in giving the sponsor's kid the first shot at pitching?" Kristy demanded. "You would've had your chance after a couple of games! But no! You went mental city — screaming at me, and even dissing my main man P.P. That's why you didn't pitch back *then*. But when you wrote that letter to Mr. Lopez, you could've gotten P.P. *fired*!"

I studied the carpet. I guess I never thought about making trouble for the professor — just Kristy!

She folded her arms in front of her. "It would've broken his heart! So I made up my mind — the seas would dry up, chickens would grow lips, and Mickey Mouse would get his face on Mount Rushmore before you got to pitch."

My guts were churning. An entire summer in left field! Two months of rage and frustration! And now I was supposed to believe it was all my own fault!

It was *so* unfair. Picture this: The neighbors' dog howls all night, you yell at him to shut up, and the police arrest *you* for disturbing the peace. That's how I felt. I made a legitimate complaint to try to help the team, and I got killed.

There was no justice — none except that the season was over, and I wouldn't have to think about this anymore.

Professor Pendergast was on the phone, a confused expression on his face. When he hung up, he was grave. "Attention everybody. I have some bad news. I just spoke to the umpire-in-chief. He says we aren't finished after all."

Mr. Featherstone regarded him in perplexity. "But the season's over."

"That's what I told him," replied the professor. "He said we have to play some more games."

"But there *aren't* any more games!" blurted Ernie.

The professor looked thoughtful. "It has something to do with a mumps epidemic. The Dodgers all have it. Which means we have to play these extra games — I forget what he called them."

"Playoffs?" I cried out.

Our coach snapped his fingers in recognition. "Right. The playoffs. I'm sorry," he added.

With a lightning motion, Kristy snapped the giant sandwich out of Tuba Dave's hands. "Hit the crabgrass, pal. This season's not over yet!"

CHAPTER ◇ 9 ◇

Pitcher —
Kevin Featherstone

Our most loyal fan was our sponsor, Mr. Featherstone. Here he was, a hardworking businessman, president of a company, but he always found the time to come out to the park and cheer us on.

Not that Feather-Soft Bathroom Tissue Inc. was like IBM, or some huge corporation like that. It was just a little factory in downtown Spooner. And they didn't make normal toilet paper; they made designer stuff — flowers, family crests, initials, and forest scenes. It really was as soft as feathers. I made my mom buy it, out of team loyalty. It falls apart in your hand! It's as useful as a moonbeam!

Mr. Featherstone always sat in the back row of the bleachers, drenched with sweat from the climb, the heat, and the fact that he was wearing a three-piece suit.

"Come on pitch 'er in there right over the plate strike him out attaway he was out by a mile burn it in there baby watch the runner on second that was way foul easy does it ball three what're you blind ump no batter watch for the bunt way to go!"

No, that wasn't us. That was Mr. Featherstone, bellowing from the stands. Our sponsor provided jerseys, caps, equipment, and all the infield chatter you could stomach.

The best thing about Mr. Featherstone was that our team was *our team*. He never interfered. He never even made suggestions. He was just a fan and a dad.

That had been my first fight with Kristy. When she insisted Kevin had to be the pitcher because he was the sponsor's kid, I knew right then and there that she was trouble.

Kristy probably thought she could teach Kevin to pitch. After all, on the Tigers, stumblebums were turning into superstars overnight. Look at Tuba Dave, Caspar, and the twins. Somehow Kristy had figured out a way to make the most of their strengths and the least of their weaknesses.

It didn't work for Kevin. He was all weaknesses:

1. He couldn't find the plate with a map. The other teams called him the Travel Agent, because he sent so many players on trips around the bases.

2. He couldn't remember the signals.
3. He only had one pitch — the slow straight ball. If it was in your zip code, you could hit it.

Kristy nagged at him. " 'Tsupwitchoor arm? 'Tsupwitchoor eye? 'Tsupwitchoor brain?" We even trekked back out to the Crisp ranch so Kevin could throw at carnival targets. He spent hours at it, and never improved one bit. As Kristy put it, "Squat — diddly — *nada* — the hole in the dough-nut — zilcherooski!"

So he was bad. But so were the other guys. I was probably better, but I was banished from the mound, thanks to my brilliant letter to Mr. Lopez.

It explained our jitters going into the playoffs. We were a good team — *but*. Our pitching was weak, we were only there because of the mumps, and our coach thought this was all some kind of punishment handed down by the League. Plus we had to go to a field way on the other side of town. It was almost exactly like our own ballpark, right down to the parched, weedy outfield, and un-painted wooden bleachers. But to me it looked as alien as the surface of Mars.

For starters, we lost all our fans, except for the die-hard parents. We weren't supposed to be in this game, so nobody knew to come and watch us play. We barely figured it out ourselves. Three of the guys went to our own park, and Ernie somehow ended up at a dog racing track.

Mr. Rudolph was only the regular season umpire, so we were playing with a stranger behind the plate. Plus there was one extra ump who stood behind the pitcher to make the calls at the bases. He looked out of place, like some spectator who'd wandered out onto the field by mistake.

It got worse. Nobody told us there were *two* washroom huts. We tried the Devereaux switch early for Bobby Joe's extra hitting punch. But Billy Ray went to the wrong building. There he was, in the *east* washroom, wondering why he couldn't find his brother, who was waiting for him in the *west* washroom! And we'd gone from too many players to not enough! We had only eight guys!

The professor went to get our shortstop, but he came back with Billy Ray again. We were pretty far behind by the time Kristy stormed the right men's room, and straightened it all out.

It didn't help. With a record of 11 and 1, the Spooner Rotary Club Giants were the second winningest team in the league. And they were pretty good, sure — but their pitcher was a real ace. He was twenty times better than me, which made him at least forty times better than Kevin. Most guys our age can manage a little curveball; this guy had a bender. The ball would be there when you started to swing, and be gone when your bat arrived. But mostly he had heat. His fastball couldn't be hit because it couldn't be seen. I never got near the ball. Our top hitters, Tuba Dave and Bobby Joe, couldn't do anything better than a few foul balls. And Caspar was worthless. No matter how he crouched and crowded the plate, the Giants star found the strike zone. After three innings, we trailed 4–zip, and that pitcher was working on a perfect game.

If you think we were frustrated, you should have seen Kristy. "Look at him!" she raged. "He's a nerd! His hat's too big! His socks are drooping! *He's not even from New York!*"

"Yeah, but did you see that fastball?" breathed Tim.

"No," said Tuba Dave honestly. "I haven't seen anything leave his hand all day."

"We're never going to hit that guy!" Ernie sighed. "It's impossible. This is our last game."

Kristy held up her hands for order. "Let's take a group chillathon. Mellow on the moaning. Lose the loser talk. *Get a grip!* Sure, he's a good pitcher. He's terrific. But we've got something even better."

"A bazooka?" asked Luis.

Kristy ignored him, and held up a glass bottle. The label read: MAGNIFICENT PICKLE COMPANY.

"Oh, wow," I said sarcastically. "An empty jar."

"It's not empty," she countered. "I took it over to the particle accelerator last night." Her voice dropped. "There's a lepton in here."

We all looked. I have no idea what we expected to see.

"There's nothing," said Ernie.

Tuba Dave elbowed him in the ribs. "Don't you know anything? You can't see a lepton!"

"Wow!" breathed Ernie. He looked puzzled. "What good is it?"

"Every great team has a lucky charm that makes them unbeatable," lectured Kristy. "Like homer hankies, or the tomahawk chop, or pyramid power. Hockey players stop shaving for the playoffs. Whole basketball teams put their shoes on left foot first. Did you know that the Chicago Bears are undefeated on odd-numbered days when the quarterback wears boxer shorts with a picture of Mount McKinley on them?"

"If it works for the pros, it can work for us!" cried Ernie.

"Aw, come on!" I protested. "It's nothing but superstition!"

"Yo, bro'," said Kristy. "Some of the greatest athletes in the world are superstitious. Now, all you have to do is focus the energy of the lepton into your bats."

I was next in the order, and I had to stand there while she held that empty pickle jar over my head, and then ran it along the end of the bat. The Giants were staring into our dugout. It was the most humiliating experience of my life.

"This jar stinks!" I complained. "I'll bet you found it in the garbage ten minutes ago!"

"Get out there, Johnson!" she ordered. "You're a lean, mean hitting machine."

I took my place at the plate. "I'm going to hit a home run," I informed the catcher bitterly. "I've got lepton power."

"Strike!" My lepton power didn't even see the first pitch.

"Strike two!"

I looked to our dugout. Every eye was upon me. Kristy was pointing that stupid pickle jar like a ray gun. Did she think we were all morons?

The pitcher wound up and the ball left his hand. I don't know what made me close my eyes. I just knew I could never time a pitch that fast, so I might as well swing blindly, and get it over with.

CRACK!

My shoulders jarred as the bat made contact. I opened my eyes to see the ball soaring away from me. There was no fence in this park, but that ball sailed high over the outfielders' heads, across the street, and straight down an open manhole.

When I trotted triumphantly back to the dugout, I found my teammates lined up, waiting for Kristy to hold that stupid pickle jar over their heads.

"Aw, come *on*!" I protested. "A lepton didn't hit that home run! *I* did!"

"Sure!" said Ernie. "Because you had lepton power!"

I didn't even get credit for my one home run. "We all know there's nothing in that jar," I said weakly. "And even if there was, how would it make you a better baseball player?" But my protests fell on deaf ears, especially when Kevin, our worst player, got a single. Then Caspar, at the top of the order, managed a walk.

Kristy grinned at me. "What do you say to that, bro'?"

I grasped at straws. "Maybe their pitcher's getting tired. Or rattled. Maybe he's starting to lose confidence."

"Or?" she prompted.

"Or maybe he's only good for three innings. Or maybe the catcher's calling the wrong signals."

"Or?" she persisted.

"Or maybe there's a lepton in that idiot pickle jar!" I howled in surrender. No, I didn't believe it. But neither did anybody else, *really*.

By the middle of the fourth, we had cut the lead to 4–3. I was almost happy when the Giants scored another run. At least it proved that pickle jar wasn't perfect!

Kevin threw down his glove. "I don't get it," he

said. "Maybe I've been holding the jar wrong."

We whittled the lead down to 5–4, but with Billy Ray in the washroom hut, Bobby Joe was at short, so our defense was weak. It was a miracle that we only gave up one more run to trail 6–4.

"Stay loose," Kristy advised, rubbing the pickle jar on Bobby Joe's bat. "Relax your muscles, and let the lepton do the rest."

I watched in disbelief as the lepton scored three runs. I couldn't explain it to save my life. Their pitcher was still great, but we were swinging at those super-fastballs with confidence and authority. And not just our big guns, either. Luis, Ryan, and Ernie all recorded hits against the ace of the League.

Then we went into the bottom of the sixth to protect our 7–6 lead. This was the worst part of being the visiting team. Since the Giants were up last, the game was really theirs to win. We couldn't get any more runs, but we could give some up. It was nail-biting time.

The leadoff man hit a triple. Two walks later, I was dying. With the bases loaded, the winning run was on second, and there were no outs yet!

Then Caspar pounced on a grounder, and fired it home for the force-out. Luis sizzled it to first to complete a tough double play. We still had the lead, with runners on second and third.

But with Kevin pitching, an empty base didn't

stay that way for long. Four balls later, they were loaded again.

The Giants' captain came to bat. He took three balls, and it looked like Kevin was about to walk in the tying run. I'm sure the signal must have been for no swing, but Kevin served him a pitch *nobody* could pass up.

He crushed it. It flew so high that we lost it in the clouds. When it reappeared, it was heading straight down the middle, and it was a home run for sure.

I cried out, *"Deep center!"* and Tim was sprinting backward, but this one was headed for Louisiana. The bases cleared as, one by one, four Giants crossed the plate.

Our season was over, and everybody knew it except Tim Laredo. From the curb at the edge of the field, he launched himself wildly upward. I thought he was a dead man, because he came down flat on his back into a moving convertible on the street. And the last thing I saw before Tim and the car disappeared down the road was this beautiful glint of white ball against brown mitt.

"You're out!" bellowed the field umpire.

And the Tigers were in the final!

The owner of the convertible charged Mr. Featherstone for the cleat marks on his bucket seats. Our sponsor was happy to pay up.

◇

There never was such a Cinderella story. There we were, the rejects of the League, the leftovers the professor got because he forgot to go to the draft meeting. We didn't have a coach — not a real one, anyway; we had to put up with a crazy New Yorker who just wouldn't leave us alone; we lived with the constant threat of The Picture and public humiliation; we were misfits — a catcher who was afraid of the ball, an overeater, a summer school dropout, a workaholic, a figure skater, a victim, a guy who was really two guys, a pitcher who couldn't pitch, and me, stranded out in left field. And most of them ready to put all their faith in a subatomic particle in a pickle jar! In three days, *this* would be playing in the championship game!

During the wild victory celebration, I pulled the professor aside and asked him if it was possible to catch a lepton. He laughed like crazy, and said, "That's a good one. Now I've got a joke for you. How many quantum physicists does it take to screw in a lightbulb?"

I don't remember the answer.

The plan was to take Thursday off, with a final practice Friday, and the big game Saturday at one.

I *needed* that day off. The sheer excitement of

who we were, and where we were going was driving me nuts. I alternated between joy and misery, the thrill of victory and the deep-rooted feeling that it was all a mistake, and we didn't belong, and disaster was just around the corner.

Everything reminded me of baseball — the posters on my wall were all pitchers; my dad wore his Astros cap to cut the grass; our aluminum siding matched my favorite bat. I couldn't even escape it in Spooner Park. All the birds seemed to be orioles, cardinals, and blue jays — the baseball birds.

I sat in the tunnel part of the big jungle gym. It didn't help. Kristy tracked me down anyway.

" 'Tsup? Hibernation City, man. C'mon. We're late for the game."

"What game?" I growled.

"The dodgeball game at the nursery school!" she shot back. "Get with the program, Johnson! The other semifinal! Wouldn't it be nice to have an idea of who we're playing on Saturday?"

I shrugged. "The coach is supposed to do that . . ." My voice trailed off. Okay. For the team, and *only* for the team, I would allow myself to be in the company of this rotten backstabber. But after Saturday's game, she no longer counted as a life-form!

We went to the same field as our own semifinal. But there seemed to be a lot more interest in this game. The bleachers were jam-packed. We squeezed into a back-row bench behind third base.

"Aren't you going to take notes?" I muttered.

"No paper, bro'," Kristy replied.

"So what's in there?" I indicated the enormous shopping bag she'd lugged from home.

It was crammed full of food — sandwiches, chips, cake, popcorn, pretzels, candy, and a six-pack of Coke. She stretched out, elbowing the man next to her until he gave way and made room. And then she watched the game, munching, and swigging soda. I got a nibble in here and there, but as the innings progressed, my appetite left me.

It wasn't a game; it was a massacre. The Raiders were sponsored by East Texas Demolition, and there was a lot of that going on. They were big, they were mean, they were tough — half of them had mustaches! They hit like monsters, fielded like precision machines, and strutted around like they owned the world. They did. Most Little League teams attracted relatives and friends. The Raiders had *fans*! Real fans! Strangers! Hundreds of them! Baseball nuts who put their hearts and souls behind the best Little League team they'd ever seen!

The Raiders looked unbeatable. They had signals the CIA couldn't figure out! They had coaches at first and third! They had relief pitchers in the bull-pen — not that the starting guy needed any help! It was already 8–0, and they were only in the third inning! Their opponents were pretty good, too — fourth best in the league. Nobody had to get the mumps for them to make the playoffs! Yet they were getting smashed. I thought of Saturday and went cold all over.

"I'm feeling kind of woozy," I told Kristy.

She held out a chicken leg. "Chow down."

"Aren't you watching?" I raved.

"Sure. Hype game. A little one-sided."

"One-sided?!" I howled. "We can't play those guys! They're *pros!*"

"We've got lepton power," she mumbled, mouth full.

"Could we trade it in for *nuclear* power?" I asked bitingly. " 'Cause if we can't, you should be praying, not stuffing your face!"

The Raiders steamrolled on, ringing up runs like a cash register. By the time the bloodletting was over, it was 14–0. The crowd roared its approval, but I was very quiet.

On the way out, we ran into, of all people, the professor! What a great guy. Who would believe he was related to that miserable Kristy? Even though he knew nothing about baseball, he had come to do his job as coach and scout the game.

"What did you learn, Grandpa?"

The professor put on his reading glasses and flipped open his notebook. "They're not very strong," he reported. "They didn't get any runs to-day, while allowing a great many — "

Inside, I turned to stone. Our coach had scouted the wrong team!

"But, Grandpa," Kristy interrupted. "Those are the losers. They're eliminated. We need information on the other team."

"Ah, yes, the other team," he said thoughtfully, and fell silent as he searched his mind for his impressions. "Well — they had hats." He brightened. *"We* have hats! I predict an even contest!"

And you had to take it as gospel truth from a man who couldn't tell the winners from the losers in a 14–0 blowout.

CHAPTER 10

Left Field — Corey Johnson

The championship game was scheduled for one o'clock at Legion Field, a small park on the outskirts of Dallas. The Professor was picking me up at ten. I was ready at 7:03.

I never thought of myself as a nervous person, but by eight-thirty, I was sitting on my gym bag in the driveway. I'd already phoned the coach three times, but I kept getting Kristy. Now I was following her advice. I was chilling. In East Texas in August, this is impossible.

They picked me up last. I was a wreck. The rest of the guys were pumped up, but kind of loose and relaxed. They passed around the lepton jar, rubbing it carefully.

"This isn't the way to Dallas," I pointed out as the professor took an unfamiliar turn.

"I've got a special treat," our coach announced. "I know a shortcut; and it takes us right by the particle accelerator, so you can see where I work."

"Maybe we can get another lepton!" exclaimed Ernie.

The professor laughed. "You boys are full of fun. We're going to have a wonderful day." And we all cheered as he turned onto County Road 5416.

"Johnson and I checked out the Raiders," announced Kristy. "They're *nothing*. Right, Johnson?"

I almost fell out of the van. "Oh — yeah, sure. Nothing." Nothing short of invincible.

"I wonder how they made it to the final," mused Billy Ray.

"It was a fluke," Kristy snorted. Then she had the *nerve* to launch into a lecture about how, when playing a weaker team, you have to watch out for overconfidence. *Overconfidence* against the undefeated number-one team in the league!

I glared at Kristy. Through clenched teeth I whispered, "Don't you think they're going to notice when we're down 40–zip?"

"Take a chill-pill."

About twenty minutes later, we passed the particle accelerator. At least, the professor said we did. All I could see was a fifteen-foot electrified barbed-wire fence, with signs about attack dogs in eight different languages.

"What do you think, boys?" asked the professor proudly.

"They love it," Kristy answered for us. "Grab some Z's, dudes. Absolutely nothing can keep us from winning the championship!"

And with that, the van died. No rattle, no smoke, not so much as a cough. The professor didn't even have time to pull over to the side. We just passed out on County Road 5416, too far from home to walk back, too far from the Interstate to get help.

Our coach tried the key. There wasn't so much as a sputter. Get this: Professor Pendergast, Ph.D. in physics, needed help to find the hood release. Of course, once the hood was up, he stood there and stared at all that silent machinery.

"What's wrong with it, Grandpa?" asked Kristy.

"I have absolutely no idea," said the world-renowned genius.

"But I thought you knew all about science," said Tuba Dave.

"I only know about very, very small things," our coach explained. "This engine alone must be a billion billion times bigger than a lepton."

The Devereaux twins peered at the ailing engine.

"Uh-oh," said Billy Ray.

"Uh-oh," agreed Bobby Joe.

"What's the tip?" Kristy demanded.

"The distributor cap is split," said Billy Ray. "We're not going anywhere."

There was an uneasy murmur from the team.

Tim snapped his fingers. "Let's go get help at your office, Professor!"

"Oh, but my office is forty miles away," said our coach.

"I thought you worked at the particle accelerator," said Ernie.

"I do. But the particle accelerator is a big circle, a hundred and ten miles around."

No way! I always thought it was a *machine,* the size of a dishwasher, or something!

We were so shocked that it took a few seconds for us to realize we were totally out of touch. To our left, deserted range; to our right, a one-hundred-and-ten-mile-long electric fence.

Kevin was the first to panic. "If we can't get there by game time, we lose automatically!"

"Against a team we could beat *easy!*" added Bobby Joe.

"I ate all that crabgrass for nothing!" mourned Tuba Dave.

"What a bunch of hicks!" sighed Kristy in disgust. "A little engine trouble, and you're having a freak-orama! P.P. and I'll flag down the next car, and ride back to Spooner for some wheels! So C — H — I double hockey sticks!"

Half an hour later, not one single car had come along in either direction.

"Where are our parents?" wailed Ernie. "They

169

have to drive by us to get to the game!"

"Not if they take the Interstate!" growled Tuba Dave. "We're out by the particle accelerator!"

"Northeast sector," supplied the professor, playing tour guide. "Not far from where the antilepton was recorded."

Even Kristy was showing signs of stress. "What kind of a stupid, unchill, wack place *is* this?" she raved, her face a thundercloud. "Where are all the people? In New York, eight hundred taxis would have gone by! The van would be stripped naked! We'd all be arrested for loitering!"

Her voice was the only sound. It was eerie.

There we sat, cross-legged on the shoulder, stretched out in the grass, draped over the van. It was the worst moment of everybody's life. Even if a high-speed train pulled up to take us express to the ballpark, we'd still be cutting it close. It was almost noon!

We had come so far, only to lose by default in a ditch in the middle of nowhere. Suddenly, I understood those Olympic athletes, who train for years only to finish dead last, and still say, "I'm happy just to be here!" Sure, we were probably going to lose anyway. But we had the right to *be there,* to play in a championship game!

Something in me must have snapped. I got up out of the ditch, and marched into the van like a robot guided by remote control. Even then, part of me knew it was stupid. But I picked up that empty pickle jar, and I put it on my head.

"Okay, lepton, I'm not asking just for myself. We *need* to make that ballgame! Please! *Please! PLEASE!*" I peered out the windshield. Out of the heat shimmer at the vanishing point of the highway, a black shape appeared.

The others jumped up, eyes fixed on the horizon. I squinted at the approaching dust cloud until I could make out the form in front of it. My jaw dropped in horror. It was a black-jacketed motor-cycle gang, coming up *fast*!

I watched, transfixed, as Kristy Pendergast stepped fearlessly out into the middle of the road. She stood there, directly in the path of all that hurtling, roaring machinery, raised her right arm, and bellowed, *"YO!"*

I don't buy all this New York stuff, but I've got to say that nobody in Spooner could have done that.

They didn't slow down.

Kristy never flinched.

At the last second, the leader braked hard. The others squealed into formation behind him in a cloud of burning rubber. They looked like cavemen on wheels, and they weren't too happy about leaving half their tire treads on the road. Their leather jackets said TIGERS OF TERROR. The leader growled; I think it was speech. The others just glared at Kristy, and revved their engines.

Kristy grinned broadly. " 'Tsup?" she greeted. "How'd you like to help out some fellow Tigers?"

I rode on the back of a 2000 cc Harley, with a guy named Sawdust. It's not easy hanging onto a chopper doing ninety-five, while trying to balance a duffel bag full of baseball bats. But I would have done it standing on my head, juggling flaming swords. We were late, but we were on our way.

Kristy was riding up front with the gang leader, Shlomo. The Professor was with Shlomo's girl-friend, Crusher, who thought he was kind of cute. And the rest of the team was portioned out among the fifty or so riders of the Tigers of Terror, East Texas Branch.

I don't know why they helped us. Kristy didn't have pictures of any of *them* in their jockstraps. It was probably the way she got everything done. She wouldn't shut up, and the only way to get on with your life was to do what she wanted. Plus they had to have respect for a twelve-year-old girl who could flag down a motorcycle gang like she was hailing a cab on Broadway.

So the Tigers of Terror brought the Tigers of Toilet Paper to our date with destiny. Thirty-nine minutes later, we roared onto the field, just in the nick of time. Mr. Featherstone and Mrs. Jablonski were on their way to their cars to search for us. Luis's mom was at a pay phone, probably calling the State Police to put out an A.P.B. on a lost baseball team. All our parents looked pretty frazzled. It was a combination of relief that we showed up, and shock at who we showed up *with*.

The umpires were counting off minutes. Ninety seconds later would have meant a forfeit. You can't get much closer than that.

The Little League crowd wasn't thrilled with our method of transportation. Fifty-odd bikers made a pretty fearsome sight in a suburban neighborhood, especially when they didn't leave. The Tigers of Terror took over a section of bleachers, and settled in to watch the game.

We got no batting practice, and no warm-up. Instead, they gave us two minutes to change. We did it in one. The twins didn't even need a bathroom to hide in. In this park, each team had its own clubhouse in the back of the dugout.

On my way to left field, it hit me. We were sending Kevin — *Kevin* — to pitch to East Texas Demolition. 12 and 0, not including their semifinal blowout. The Tigers had maybe two dozen fans in the whole stadium. Everyone else was there to see the Raiders murder us.

My stomach was very tight as I watched the

group of gorilla-size Little Leaguers in their dugout. There was a lot of confident backslapping and joking around. Finally, a gorilla with 33 on his uniform came out to lead off.

It took exactly one pitch. The CRACK! sounded like he broke the stadium. The ball sailed high over my head, and number 33 trotted around the bases.

Tim called to me from center, "I think that's the kid who won the Little League batting title."

The next two guys must have been the runners-up, because they added a single each. And just when it seemed that things couldn't get any worse, they did! I squinted into the dugout.

Kristy was flashing the signal for the old hidden ball trick. She always made us practice it, but I never thought she'd be stupid enough to try it in a game.

Luis called time, and the whole infield had a conference on the mound.

I waved my arms and tried to call her off. The old hidden ball trick hadn't worked in fifty years! Bad enough that the Raiders were going to kill us! Now Kristy was setting us up to look like clowns!

Even from left field, it was obvious. Kevin slipped the ball to Tuba Dave, and the infielders went back to their positions. Kevin tried to pretend that he was about to start pitching again. The idea of this tired old play was that, when the guy on second took his lead, Tuba Dave could pull out the hidden ball, and tag him off base.

Everybody knew. The runner on second was laughing. In the Raiders' dugout, they were rolling on the floor. Spectators in the last row of bleachers were onto us. If the Goodyear Blimp had been up there, the pilot would have looked down and said, "Oh, it's the old hidden ball trick."

Finally, we had to humiliate ourselves further. Tuba Dave waddled back to the mound and slipped Kevin the ball. Everybody saw that, too.

On our side, the only infielder who deserved to be on the same field as East Texas Demolition was Billy Ray. And the humiliation of the failed trick must have really smarted, because he stepped up his game with some brilliant diving stops. Even with his amazing play, we gave up another run. We were lucky to get out of the inning down only 2–0.

"We've got 'em on the ropes!" Kristy assured us as we dragged ourselves into the dugout and prepared for our at bat.

That was over all too quickly, because their pitcher made short work of our guys. The only Tiger to get a hit was Tuba Dave. With two outs, he got the brilliant idea to steal second. It got an even bigger laugh than the old hidden ball trick.

The Raiders were destroying us, but they always seemed to strand a lot of men on base. So we were only behind 3–0 when I first came to bat in the bottom of the second. Nobody was panicking yet as we rubbed our bats with the pickle jar.

Their pitcher wasn't as tough as the ace from our semifinal, but he was the only Little Leaguer I've ever seen who could throw knuckleballs. Hitting a knuckleball is like chasing a butterfly. You never know what it's going to do. I took a mighty cut and hit a screaming foul liner. It sliced right into our dugout. I could see the guys diving in all directions. And then . . .

Crash! Tinkle!

I ran over there to see if everyone was okay. Nobody was moving. They were scattered like tenpins, their faces white as chalk. I followed their staring eyes to the center of the bench. There sat a little pile of broken glass with a baseball in the middle of it. The lid was on the dugout floor — MAGNIFICENT PICKLE COMPANY.

Ernie was the first to react. "Our lepton!" he wailed, sifting through the pieces of shattered glass. Like he was going to find a lepton just sitting there in the dugout!

"It's gone!" said Tuba Dave mournfully.

Luis looked at me reproachfully. "You lost our lepton."

Professor Pendergast had just heard the one word that could bring him out of his usual baseball coma. "Lepton? What's all this about a lepton?"

"We had a lepton in the jar," Tim explained, "and Corey broke it, and now it got away."

The professor smiled indulgently. "Boys, boys, whoever told you that you could keep a lepton in a jar? A lepton is so tiny that it would slip right between the glass molecules. Besides, leptons only exist for a fraction of a second."

We all glared at Kristy. There was a long silence.

"All right, there wasn't any lepton," she admitted finally. "I found the jar in the garbage, like Johnson said. But don't you see what that means? That was *you* last game, not any power, or magic, or lucky charm! *You* beat those guys! *You* got seven runs off the best pitcher in Little League! We're here today because of *you*! You're my *posse*!"

"Posse?" queried Caspar.

"You know. My squad, my dudes, my boys, my homeys. My *team*!" she translated.

"What's the delay here?" came a voice from the field. A tall, dark man stood there, bending over to peer into our dugout.

"Yo, bub, this is a private team meeting!" snapped Kristy. "Buzz off!"

The man was taken aback. "Are you Kristy Pendergast?"

Kristy frowned. "Who wants to know?"

The man glared at her. "I happen to be Jack Lopez, president of this league." He turned to the professor sternly. "Pendergast, I forwarded you a complaint about this girl, but it's obvious she's still causing problems within the team. Why haven't you resolved the situation?"

The professor was struck dumb. He regarded Mr. Lopez, then his granddaughter, then Mr. Lopez again. "Uhhhhhh — "

The league president didn't wait for an answer. He turned to Kristy. "Young lady, I'm asking you to leave this dugout."

There was a gasp from our players.

It was the moment I'd waited for — prayed for — all season, and it was unfolding exactly the way I'd imagined it. Better, even. Not only did she have to leave us alone; she was being kicked out!

But all I could think of was . . .

"No!"

I blurted it right in the league president's face.

There was only one person in the world crazy enough to have faith in the Tigers when we were hopelessly outclassed. Suddenly, I couldn't face the rest of this game without Kristy.

"Sorry," Mr. Lopez told me, "but there's been a complaint. It's a serious matter."

"But *I* wrote the letter! And it was a mistake! I take it all back!"

"The letter was anonymous," said Mr. Lopez.

Ernie pointed at me. "That's him! *He's* anonymous!"

"He *un*-complains!" added Tuba Dave.

"I was wrong!" I babbled. "She *doesn't* push us around! I mean, she *does,* but it's all for the team! We wouldn't be here if it wasn't for her!"

Finally, the professor figured out enough to realize that his little princess was being bad-mouthed. He squared his shoulders and faced the league president.

"Sir, kindly return to your seat. We are in the middle of baseballing."

As Mr. Lopez left, Kristy put a friendly arm around my shoulders. "That was beautiful, Johnson. You're a true friend." She gave me a shove toward home plate. "Now get a hit, or never show your face around here again!"

She was obviously the sentimental type.

Back at the plate, I hit a weak grounder to third. It was an easy out, but I had to try — for the team, and even for Kristy. I put on the afterburners and blasted into first. Guess what? The throw was a little high, and the first baseman had to take his foot off the bag to catch it. Safe.

My teammates began moving me around the bases. It wasn't pretty, but it was baseball. Kevin sacrificed me to second. A knuckleball got away from the pitcher while he was searching for Caspar's tiny strike zone — I made it to third. Caspar struck out, but Tuba Dave's solid single brought me home. 3–1.

"We're *slamming!*" cheered Kristy, whatever that meant.

We had two outs on the Raiders in the top of the third when the leadoff man came up again. This time it took a whole three pitches, then POW! 4–1, East Texas Demolition.

We bounced back. Caspar finally got himself walked and proceeded to conduct a stolen base clinic. It took him two pitches to make it to third. He took huge leads, diving back to get a finger on the bag just before the throw. It bugged the Raiders' pitcher so much that he heaved the ball over the third baseman's head, trying to pick Caspar off. Caspar strolled home, and that was it for the starter. A relief pitcher came in to get the Raiders out of the inning, still ahead, 4–2.

For a team like us to stay with East Texas Demolition, we have to be perfect. And you just can't keep that up for a whole game. Fatigue made us sloppy. With only one out in the fourth, Billy Ray made an error on a routine ground ball. And it felt like, if a player *that good* could make a play *that bad* in a game *this big,* then surely none of the rest of us could do anything right. We fell apart. Ryan lost a fly ball in the sun, and then Luis let a pitch get away from him. And all of a sudden the bases were loaded. Kevin got spooked and walked in a run. And we all wanted to die.

From the dugout, Kristy fired a stream of New

Yorkese about "being cooler than cool," but we were caving in.

Suddenly, a volley of cries from the stands reached us. "Come on Tigers! You can do it!"

"These guys can't hit! Pitch it in there!"

"Strike 'im out!"

It wasn't our parents. And everyone else in the park was there to see the Raiders kick butt. I searched the crowd. Where did we get fans so far from home? And then I saw them — our motorcycle gang, the Tigers of Terror. Sawdust, Crusher, Shlomo, and the boys — they were on their feet, chanting, *"Here we go, Tigers, Here we go!"* (Stomp! Stomp!)

The Raiders' boosters were staring at them — fifty voices drowning out an entire stadium.

It sounded great and felt even better. It put the fires of hope back into Feather-Soft Bathroom Tissue Inc.

Billy Ray redeemed himself by scooping up a tricky grounder. The double play went shortstop to second to first. That got us back up to bat. We pulled the big Devereaux switch, adding Bobby Joe's offensive power to the order. The timing was perfect. The Raiders had already pegged Billy Ray as a lightweight, so the pitcher wasn't too careful with his lookalike. Bobby Joe smashed the first pitch into the gap in center field and went into third base standing up. Luis sacrificed him home. 5–3.

The Tigers of Terror were dancing in the aisles.

We outfielders got a workout in the fifth. Everything Kevin threw was smashed back at us a country mile. Tim saved a sure triple by literally climbing the center field wall to pull in the ball. In right, Ryan had to sprint forward to make a diving catch for a short pop that was too far out for Tuba Dave. The next blast came to me. At the last second, I realized I'd misjudged the hit. Desperately, I threw my bare hand up, and felt the ball smack into my palm. The force carried me into the wall, but I held on, giddy with exultation — three up, three down.

Our big hitters were finally starting to click. In the bottom of the fifth, Tim and Tuba Dave both came through with singles, and the Raiders' coaches yanked the pitcher and put in their closer to face Bobby Joe.

This kid threw sidearm, with his release a foot off the ground, sending a projectile that looked like it was coming at you from an underground launcher. The first pitch sizzled in at waist level. Bobby Joe swung mightily. But by the time the bat got there, the ball was up at his shoulders. Strike one. The next came screaming in two inches off the ground, so our big hitter didn't swing. But suddenly, the ball rose sharply to cross the plate just above the knees. Strike two.

In the dugout, Kristy turned to me. "He's gonna hit a dinger."

I frowned. "What's a dinger?"

The third pitch was a wobbler nowhere near the plate. But Bobby Joe was sick of this game, and he reached for it. He made solid contact right at the end of the bat, pulling to the left to keep it fair. Nobody jumped for this one. It was over the moon.

Kristy turned to me. *"That's* a dinger."

I hardly heard her. We were screaming ourselves hoarse as Tim, Tuba Dave, and finally Bobby Joe crossed the plate. Our motorcycle gang was going berserk. Sawdust and Shlomo had climbed down the back of the bleachers, and were involved in a footrace for the home run souvenir. Most important of all, the Feather-Soft Tigers had our first lead of the game, 6–5. We were three outs away from the championship. Everything rested on . . .

". . . on Kevin," Kristy was saying.

Our celebration died abruptly. Kevin looked sick.

"If you shut them down here, there won't *be* a bottom of the sixth," she reminded him. "So don't choke."

He choked. He hit the first batter on the leg, then gave up a double that put runners on second and third. Four balls later, the bases were loaded, with nobody out. A pop fly would bring in the tying run; a single would put us behind again; a (gulp) home run would give the Raiders a 9–6 lead. We'd never come back from that!

I squinted in from left field, and almost wept. The

guy up there, swinging a bat that looked like a telephone pole, was none other than number 33, the Little League batting champion!

◇

Kristy was out talking with Kevin and Luis. They seemed to agree on something, and suddenly they were beckoning me in. Why me? Who calls in the left fielder for a conference on the mound? Did they think I'd have some super strategy that would get us out of this no-win situation?

I jogged in and joined them. "What's going on?"

In answer, Kristy pressed the ball into my hand, and started back to the dugout. Luis headed for the plate, and Kevin was on his way to left field!

I nearly choked. She was expecting me to pitch! *Now!* When we had *no chance!* She didn't want a pitcher; she wanted a goat! It was her final revenge for my letter to Mr. Lopez! I was going to be the guy who threw the pitch that sank the Tigers!

"How can you do this to me?" I howled.

She wheeled to face me, eyes flashing. "Isn't that just like a rural dude! All season you've been sweating me about how you're this hype pitcher."

"Yeah, but — "

"But nothing! This is your *dream,* Johnson! How many of us ever get the chance to spit back the reality sandwich?" She pointed a casual thumb in

184

the direction of big number 33. "Throw this guy curveballs."

I was in a daze. "What?"

"Curveballs," she repeated. "You *do* have a curveball?"

"Of course I do!" I said indignantly.

Shakily, I threw a few warm-ups. They'd give me as much time as I needed, coming in cold like that. But how could it make up for an entire season of not pitching? My legs were shaking. The eighty cents in my pocket jingled — everybody was looking for the ice cream man. I now understood why the big leaguers shuffle and twitch and fiddle so much. They're really putting off the pitch to the last second. If I could have delayed until next summer, it would have suited me fine.

Finally, I went into my stretch and threw a curveball. It didn't curve.

POW!

It sailed up, up, and away, and cleared the right field fence about three inches foul. The spectators let out a collective "Ooooh!"

I waited till my heartbeat returned to normal. I calmed myself — so what if it was three inches away from being a monster grand slam? It was just a strike. A very loud strike.

Breathing a silent prayer, I tried again.

POW!

This time it rocketed for left field, going, going — foul, by only *two* inches. He was getting closer.

Kristy called time, and trotted out toward me, gathering the infield for a conference on the mound. I steeled myself for the lecture. She just said, "You told me you had a curveball."

"It was about to curve," I declared defiantly, "but some guy's bat was in the way!"

"Hilarious, Johnson. Now, listen up, everybody. It's a perfect time for the old hidden ball trick."

The other guys all nodded their agreement.

I stared at her. "You're kidding."

"Chill out," she said mildly. "It's going to work."

"It *never* works!"

She shrugged. "This time there's a New York twist."

I looked to the plate. Number 33 was already laughing. The umpires were looking at their watches impatiently. In the murmur from the crowd, I only heard the words *hidden ball trick* about fifty times! Can you blame them for thinking we were idiots? Roars of laughter passed like a wave through the stadium. When we returned to our positions, we got a standing ovation.

The runners stayed on base. But wait a minute — Ernie didn't have the ball; Tuba Dave's glove was empty; and at third, Caspar was showing he had nothing. All eyes turned to Bobby Joe, but our shortstop didn't have it either. The crowd moaned its disappointment. It wasn't the hidden ball trick after all.

I pretended to go into my stance, and the runners took their leads. Suddenly, Luis rose from his crouch, pulled the ball from his mitt, and fired it down to first. The runner was watching for a throw from me, not the plate. His dive was late. Ernie tagged him out.

While this was going on, the man on third made a sprint for home. Ernie threw a perfect strike back to Luis. Our catcher caught the runner in mid-slide. It was going to be close!

"You're out!" bawled the plate umpire.

Unbelievable! Surely we were in the record book for turning the first ever old hidden ball trick double play! With a New York twist.

Number 33 wasn't laughing anymore. But he hadn't disappeared, either. And with a man on second, his big bat could put the Raiders into a tie, or even give them the lead.

Then it hit me — why not walk the guy? This kid was the Little League batting champion. With a huge foul to right and an even bigger one to left, the next ball was going dead center for sure!

I flashed a walk sign to the dugout.

No signal came back, but Kristy called out, "In your dreams, Johnson! Pitch!"

Oh, how I hated Kristy Pendergast! She'd brought us to the brink of victory, then set it up so that, if we lost it'd be *my* fault! Well, not this time! I'd pitch, all right, but first —

I turned to the infield. "You heard it! The little princess said pitch!"

The crowd was on its feet, stiff with tension. The Tigers of Terror were standing on their seats. The Raiders were all on the top step of their dugout, willing their star to hit. Our guys stood like statues at their positions, silent and scared. Kristy reclined on the bench, munching an apple, like she didn't know there was a game on.

I looked at number 33. Sure, I had two strikes on him. But how was I ever going to finish him off? Kristy wanted a curveball, but my curve wasn't curving. Maybe I should give him my fastball — or something off-speed. No, I decided. We were here because of Kristy. She'd even gotten us a ride to the game when there was no chance on Earth of us getting there. If I live to be a thousand, I'll never forget her stepping out into the road in the path of all those speeding motorcycles.

I gripped the ball by the wide seams, the way I always do for a curve. I stepped on the rubber, reared back, and let fly.

When I think back to that pitch, it all seems hazy. I see the ball in slow motion, going straight as an arrow down the alley. I hear my own voice: "Curve! *Curve!*" And I have a clear impression of what will happen if it *doesn't* curve — of number 33 blasting it into the fourth dimension. The bat comes around! The ball's still straight! And then — and then — at the last possible second, the ball makes a tiny curve, sneaks past the swinging bat, and lands with a THUMP in Luis's mitt.

"Strike three!" bellowed the umpire. "You're — !"

You couldn't hear the last word, because a motorcycle gang was storming the field in full battle cry.

Still frozen in the release position on the mound, I felt the greatest happiness of my life. The Feather-Soft Tigers came charging in from the field. I braced myself for an onslaught of joyous congratulation, but they ran straight past me. They roared into the dugout, and emerged with Kristy Pendergast on their shoulders. Not me, the hero, but Kristy! *Kristy!*

She looked down at us, her posse. "Why's everybody freaking? I told you this was going to happen." Her eyes met mine, and she grinned. "Yo, Johnson — you really *can* throw a curveball."

They presented the professor with the championship trophy. Our coach looked at the gleaming silver cup, read the words *League Champions* and, in that moment, it all came to him — a whole season of achievements that he'd missed along the way. He burst into tears. He didn't know a bat from a base, but we wouldn't have traded him for five World Series managers.

We all gathered round into a giant team bear

hug, and the Tigers of Terror joined in. They offered to drive us all the way back to Spooner. We didn't even change. We just grabbed our trophy and our stuff, hopped on the motorcycles, and began the triumphant procession home. We forgot our folks. We forgot everything but the need to stay together, and go out the way we'd come in — as a team.

I beat my parents home, so I was alone when the call came in. It was from the pay phone in the locker room at Legion Field — collect from Billy Ray.

"Is it safe to come out yet? Who won?"

EPILOGUE

The big blowout victory celebration was like New Year's Eve. I didn't get to sleep until 2 A.M. Guess who rang our doorbell at quarter to six!

Red-eyed, dazed, and exhausted, I hardly recognized Kristy. All her New York funky clothes were gone. Now she wore a DEEP IN THE ♥ OF TEXAS T-shirt, real cowboy boots, and a ten-gallon hat. Around her neck was a bolo tie with a wagon wheel on it. Her belt buckle was a lethal pair of steer horns, and her knapsack proclaimed, REMEMBER THE ALAMO, PARDNER.

"Howdy," she greeted me.

" 'Tsup?" I said, disgusted.

"Man, you look terrible. You need to sleep more."

I stood fuming in my pajamas. "What do you want?" I barked.

She shrugged. "To say good-bye, Johnson. I'm going home today."

Good-bye? Going home? It felt like Kristy had been in Spooner for a thousand years, and she'd be here for a thousand more. I guess I'd forgotten she was just visiting.

I invited her into the kitchen for some farewell cereal. "You must be pretty happy to be getting back to New York." I couldn't resist adding, "You know — the Apple, N.Y.C., Gotham, The Big Smoke, New Jack City —"

She looked at me like she'd never heard of the place. "I've got a present for you." She handed me a small envelope marked:

JOHNSON — LEFT~~FIELD~~ *PITCHER*

I was sort of embarrassed. "Gee, I didn't get you anything."

"Don't sweat it. The guys gave me tons of stuff." She indicated her all-Texas outfit.

I studied my Raisin Bran. "Sorry."

She shrugged. "You gave me something."

Team spirit? Support? "What?"

"A curveball when I really needed one."

I tore open the envelope, and gasped. Her good-bye gift was The Picture! The real McCoy! With the negative stapled to the corner!

192

There it was — the row of bare feet that she'd shown us on skating day. And above that — an extreme close-up of Kristy's finger!

I couldn't believe it! I thought back to the panic — the *terror!* — we all felt over this photograph! The ridiculous stunts we pulled to try to get the film! And Kristy had gotten her finger in front of the lens! You couldn't even see our faces! It looked like a big pink blimp with eighteen legs! She'd bamboozled us with *nothing!*

I felt my face flame. "You're really *something* — " I began angrily.

She took it as a compliment. "Thanks, Johnson. Check out the other side."

I flipped the photograph. On the back she had neatly printed:

Ms. K. Pendergast
Box 43
Bedrock Dam, NY 16902
Don't forget to write.

I frowned. "Bedrock Dam is in New York City?"
Kristy was tight-lipped. "Not exactly."

I pulled out the atlas. Bedrock Dam was nowhere near New York City! It wasn't even a town! It was a village up near the Canadian border! A tiny dot in the snow! *Half* the size of Spooner!

I looked daggers at her. "I don't know how you

have the nerve to show your face in this town! You called us hicks, hayseeds, rural dudes! You made fun of Spooner and never shut up about how much better it was in New York! And all that time, *you* were the real hick!"

She took it all good-naturedly, and even laughed at my barb about what a comedown it was going to be for her to leave the bright lights of big city Spooner.

"It was my sixth-grade field trip," she explained slowly, her eyes distant. "We went to the Statue of Liberty, and the Empire State Building. And I just *knew* New York was the place for me. The energy on the street, the pulse of the city — I was *meant* to be a New Yorker. So when I came down here where nobody knew me, and found out I'd be coaching nine dudes on a Little League team, I figured this was my big chance."

"You lied to us!" I seethed.

She shook her head. "The *real* New York's not a place, Johnson. It's an *attitude*. It doesn't matter if you're in Bedrock Dam, or Spooner, Texas, or the planet Mars. If you've got the attitude you're a New Yorker." She stood up. "I'm outta here, bro'. P.P.'s waiting to take me to the airport."

I walked her to the door, still shaking with rage. "Some New Yorker!" I seethed. "When I tell the guys — !"

"Lighten up," she laughed in my face. "You got to pitch, didn't you?"

"Oh, sure! Three pitches!"

"But in the whole season, they were the three best," she pointed out. "Later, dude."

I looked at her. "Later?"

"You know — *ciao, au revoir*, stay loose, toodle-oo, peace, *hasta la vista*. Good-bye," she translated, and was gone.

And suddenly, I was running after her, calling, "See you next summer?"

She flashed me thumbs-up and a big New York grin.

ABOUT THE AUTHOR

Gordon Korman has written over fifteen books for children and young adults, including three ALA Best Books for Young Adults: *Son of Interflux*, *A Semester in the Life of a Garbage Bag*, and *Losing Joe's Place*. When he was twelve, he wrote his first book, *This Can't Be Happening at Macdonald Hall!*, about the adventures of two friends, Bruno and Boots. He published five other books by the time he graduated from high school, and has written five other books about Bruno and Boots, most recently, *Macdonald Hall Goes Hollywood*. His latest novel, *The Twinkie Squad*, was a selection of the Junior Library Guild.

A native of Ontario, Canada, and a graduate of New York University's School of Dramatic Writing, Korman divides his time between Pompano Beach, Florida, Toronto, and New York City, and writes full time.